physiognomy (fiz i on′ o̊ mi, -og′ no̊ mi)
fisnomie, O.F. *phisonomie,* med. L. *phisonomiu, Gr.*
phusiognōmonia (*physio-, gnōmōn,* interpreter)], *n.*
The art of reading character from features of the
face or the form of the body; the face or countenance as an index of character; cast of features;
(*colloq.*) the face; the lineaments or external
features (of a landscape, etc.); aspect, appearance.

GERALD SCARFE

SINCLAIR-STEVENSON

Designed by Craig Dodd

First published in Great Britain in 1993
by Sinclair-Stevenson
an imprint of Reed Consumer Books Ltd
Michelin House, 81 Fulham Road, London SW3 6RB
and Auckland, Melbourne, Singapore and Toronto

This paperback edition published by Sinclair-Stevenson in 1994

A CIP catalogue record for this book is available
at the British Library

ISBN 1 85619 488 4

Printed and bound in Great Britain by
BPCC, Hazells Limited, Aylesbury, Bucks.

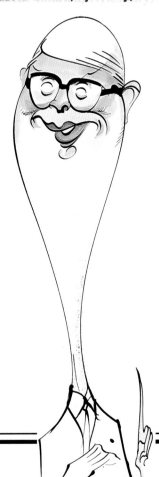

content (2) (kon' tent), *n.* Capacity or power of containing; volume; capacity; meaning; (*pl.*) that which is comprised in a vessel, writing, or book; (*pl.*) a table or summary of subject-matter.

To Alexander

Self-portrait by Alexander Scarfe at age of 11.

face (fās) [F., from pop. L. *facia*, L. *facies*], *n.* The front part of the head, the visage, the countenance; that part of anything which presents itself to the view; *v.t.* To turn the face towards; to meet in front; to confront boldly; to judge by appearances.

What is a face? Is it a collection of random features thrown together by chance, or is it formed by our experiences? Does the character flow like sap through and up the body until it unavoidably spills out onto the features like a blossoming flower? If we are what we eat, are our faces what we think? If we look shifty, were we born that way? Were we born with shifty eyes, or is it shifty behaviour that leads our eyes to move shiftily?

What can I tell from a face? The size of the nose, the shape of the ears or the colour of the hair give little indication of the whole persona. I may be able to tell the difference between a melancholic and a choleric face, but to judge character by the size of ear lobes or shape of nostrils is as nonsensical as the idea that someone with a pointed nose is likely to be in a servile position or that those with heavy jowls are of royal blood.

I judge the character of a face more by an atmosphere, an ambiance, an aroma. A succession of movements, glances, expressions. The slightest emotion, such as greed or ambition, can flicker across the face like a ripple of wind on water, giving away the deepest feelings.

The Jowel and the Crown.
The face of the cycling monarch.

The first vision that swims into focus in this world is that of a parent's face as it looms large above our crib. We look into the reassuring eyes that smile down on us and feel secure. It's our first point of contact. As we grow the face increasingly becomes the source of all information and a signal by which we know all is well – or not.

In time we learn to read every flicker of expression on our parent's face, a downturn of the mouth, a furrowing of the brows, a flash of the eyes can mean fear or happiness. So it continues into adulthood. We search the faces of those around us for information as to what they really think or feel. If they say they like us, is it true? Search the eyes: do the eyes say it or are they lying? The face is the only clue.

We may inherit facial characteristics from our parents (Ooh! Doesn't he look like you!) but that does not necessarily mean the character will be the same. The original character is independent of the face, and the face is mainly affected by what befalls that person and his reaction to it.

The face of the baby will change radically as it grows. Circumstances will change it – pain will shape it, privilege will shape it – but somewhere the original face remains. If we examine a photograph of a fifty year old man as a baby we can see the face of the grown adult already beginning to form.

Young Norman's features were all formed long before he messed up the economy.

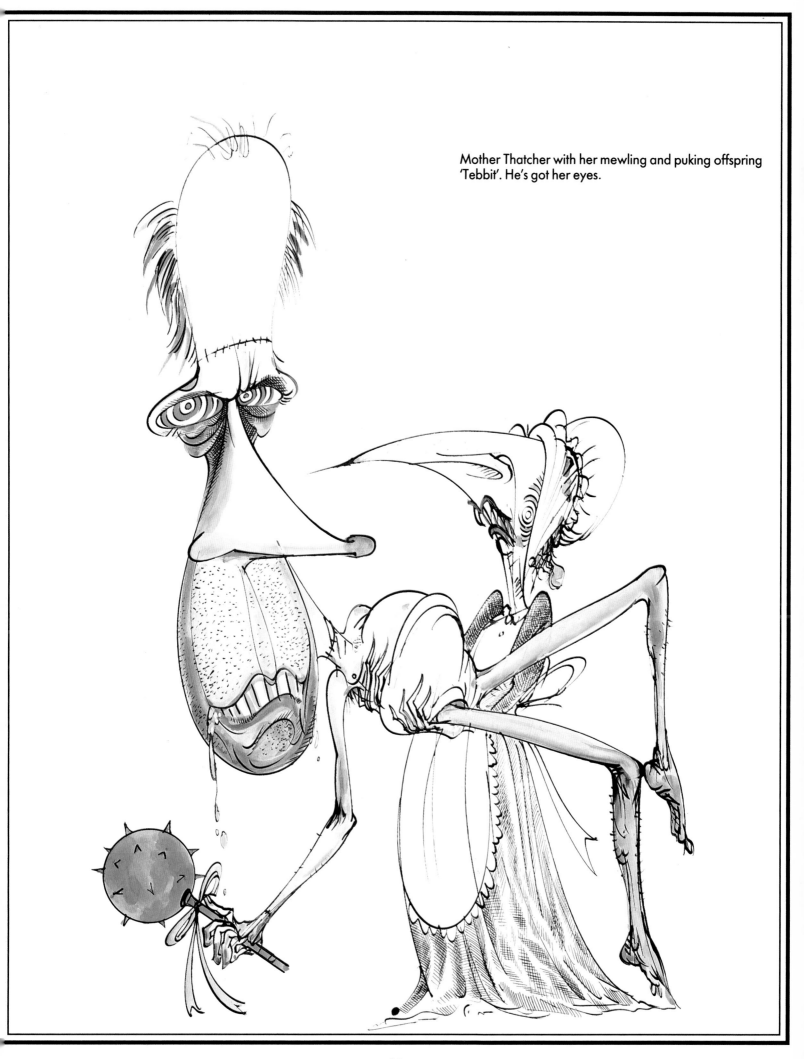

Mother Thatcher with her mewling and puking offspring 'Tebbit'. He's got her eyes.

We need the face to identify with. The terrifying head of the terrorist is all the more frightening for having no face. Nothing to give a clue of what he is thinking. Nothing with which to correspond.

Like fingerprints, no two faces are exactly the same. A face is a D.N.A. blueprint, altered by time, accident, surgery, grief or happiness. Each face is unique, and reflects our character and the passage of time and what befalls us. Even identical twins, on close examination, have different facial characteristics.

To a certain extent we create our own faces and therefore end up with the faces we deserve. A moaner's continual carping and complaining will affect his face; the muscles of the mouth will eventually form themselves in permanent preparation for bursts of pessimism. Can we keep the innermost character from marking our faces or do we get the faces we deserve? Will our thoughts, actions, morality and lifestyle mark our faces for ever?

Not always. How many times have we found that first judgments are misleading? That fellow with the awful forbidding look turns out to be quite pleasant, his expression simply a defensive mechanism hiding a nervous disposition. I have read of murder trials in the newspapers and agreed with myself that the face in the accompanying photograph was that of a real villain – anybody could see that he was a potential killer – only to find that I was looking at a photograph of the victim, not of the murderer.

Hitler did not look like a mass murderer. His face was insignificant, undistinguished, comic and forgettable – only his deeds have made him memorable, and now we see his comic face with horror. So one cannot really tell from looking at the face alone, one needs all the surrounding information.

Idi Amin

Some likenesses are fleeting impressions like tiny whispers of wind. They blow away before I can grasp them. They are there, then gone.

But others leave no doubt how they should be drawn. They might, for instance, remind me inexplicably of a fat greedy helicopter, or a strong belch of lager hitting you square between the eyes.

All of this must be captured within the spirit of a few twisting lines.

The need to simplify is purely a personal goal, saying as much as possible with economy seems to be better than smothering the subject in a spaghetti junction of lines. Some artists get away with murder, smothering their badly-constructed drawings in a great flurry of lines, effects and business. I think it fools a great many people, who feel that the more work that appears on the surface of a drawing the better it is.

Duchess of York

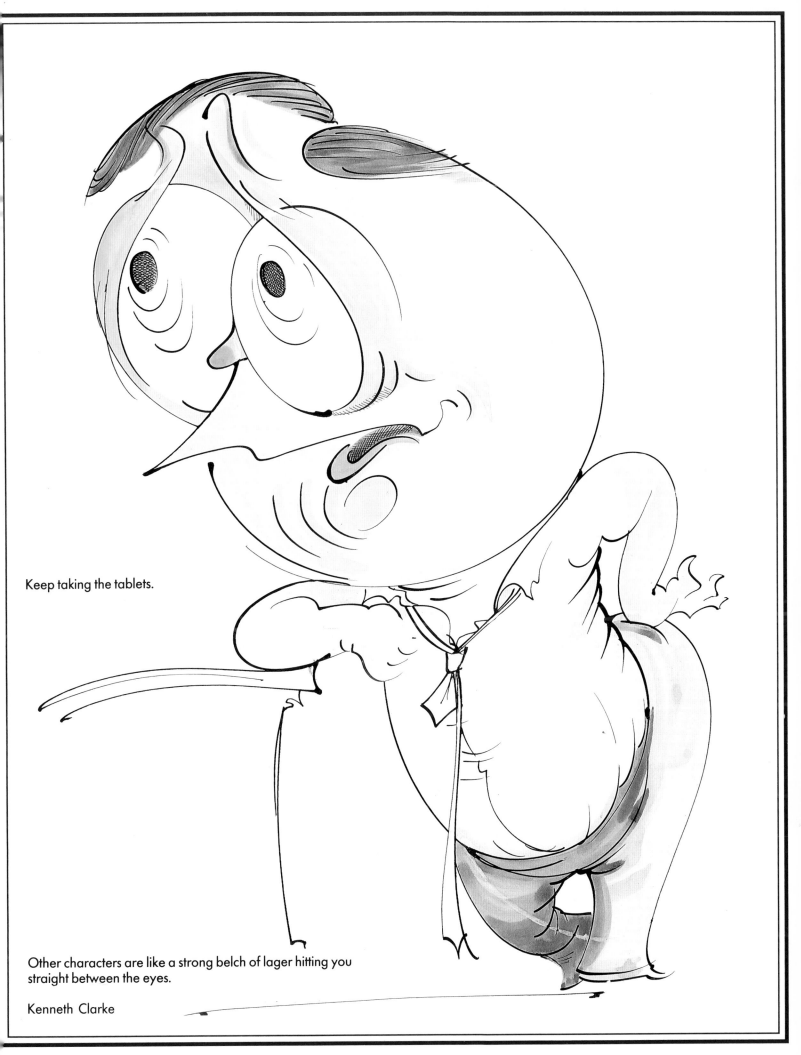

Keep taking the tablets.

Other characters are like a strong belch of lager hitting you straight between the eyes.

Kenneth Clarke

Do we know our own face? Few of us examine it in great detail. Possibly the only time we see our face is in the bathroom in the morning, trying it out in the mirror – Hello, we say, how very pleasant to meet you (devastating smile).

But the vision in the mirror is the reverse of what others see. Hair parted on the wrong side. The wrong eye higher than the other. Lopsided smile in reverse. We may, because we haven't really looked for years, see ourselves in a time warp. We take for granted the image before us without recognising how we are changing, ageing. It was a great revelation to many when they first saw themselves on video. That unfamiliar view from the back or from the side. Who is that old fogey with the saggy jowls? Oh my God! It's me.

Is it possible to disguise ourselves? Roy Strong in his days at the National Portrait Gallery seemed to me to be a collection of trendy effects beneath which it was very hard to define the true character of his face.

I suppose a Dorian Gray may exist; his portrait mouldering in some cobwebby attic as he walks the streets by day and night, his unblemished face giving no indication of his crimes.

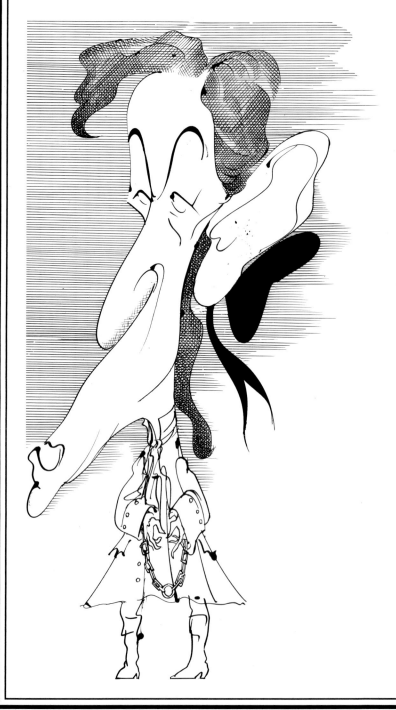

A Strong wind blows through the National Portrait Gallery.

Ian McKellen

We may see ourselves in a time warp.

What sort of face did early man have? With modern technology we can be pretty sure that he looked like Gerald Ford (the man who couldn't chew gum and walk at the same time). That same face – refined over centuries – lives today in the modern icon, Sylvester Stallone.

How has the face developed through history and do the same types of face exist through all the ages? We know by looking at portraits from Grecian times to the present that standards of beauty vary, not only from age to age but from country to country, but although the wigs, the beards, the hairstyles and the cosmetics may change, the underlying facial structure remains the same.

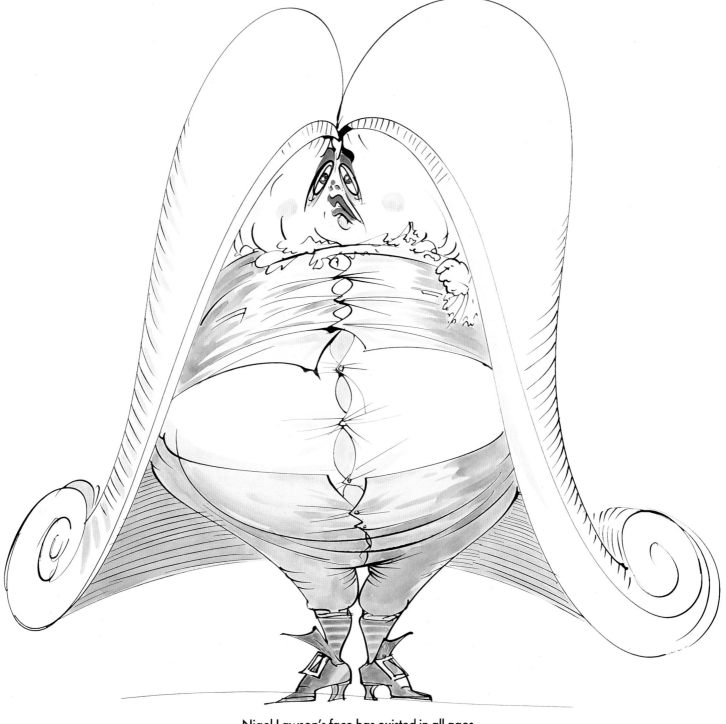

Nigel Lawson's face has existed in all ages.

Nigel Lawson, Kenneth Baker, Margaret Thatcher
1660

Nigel Lawson 1760

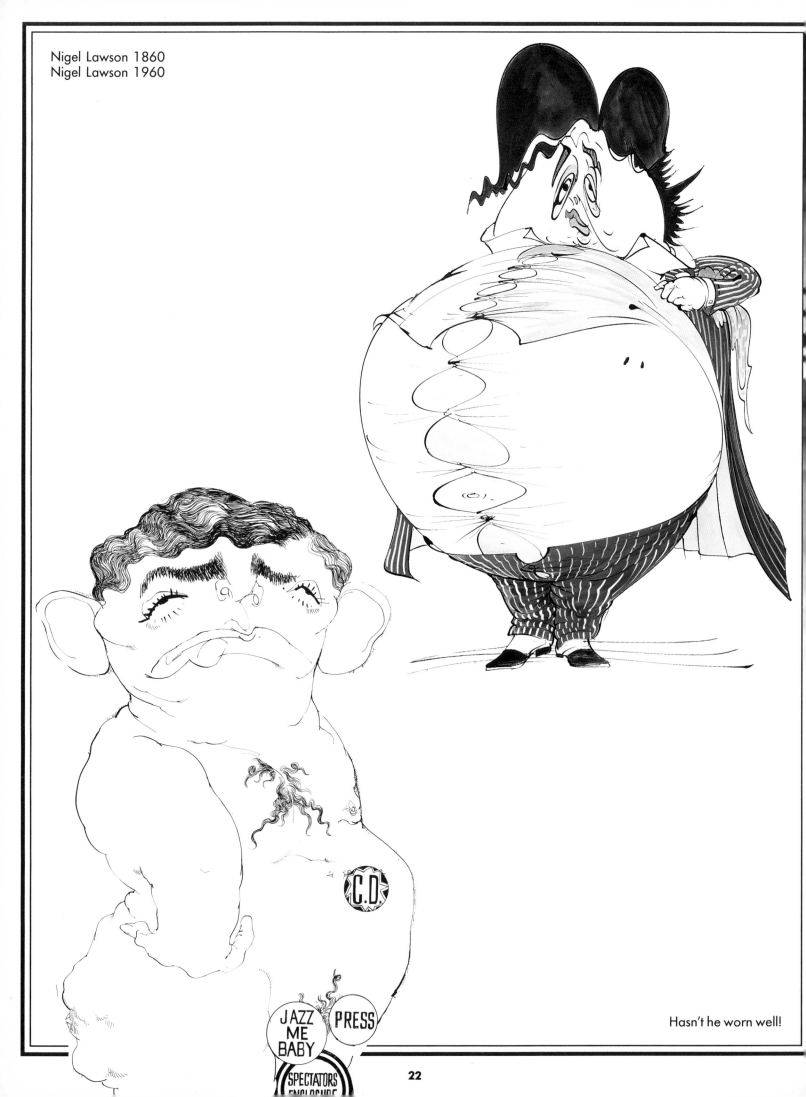

Nigel Lawson 1860
Nigel Lawson 1960

JAZZ ME BABY

PRESS

C.D.

SPECTATORS ENCLOSURE

Hasn't he worn well!

beauty (bū′ ti) [O.F. *biaute, beītet* (late L. *bellus*, see BEAU)], *n.* That quality or assemblage of qualities which gives the eye or the other senses intense pleasure; or that characteristic in a material object or an abstraction which gratifies the intellect or the moral feeling; a beautiful woman; graceful.

A modern Mona Lisa.

Standards of beauty have changed with time. How many of us really think that the Mona Lisa is beautiful today? Now beauty is to be found in the faces of Virginia Bottomley, Emma Thompson and Madonna.

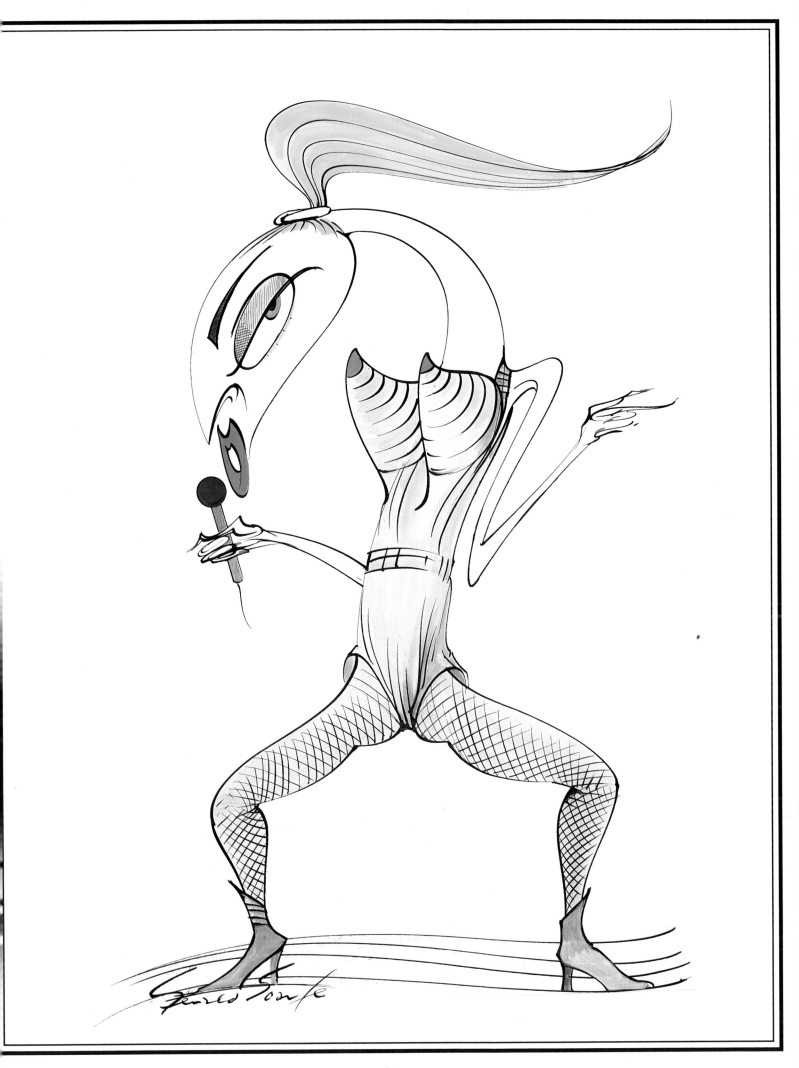

I often find the character and facial form of women difficult to define because they rarely present their true faces, enhancing them with painting and plucking. I try to draw the face as the woman herself knows it, in all its unadorned and scrubbed splendour, before I finally add the lipstick, mascara and eyebrow pencil onto the bare face in the drawing.

Joan Collins

Boy George
Clint Eastwood
Michael Heseltine

Male beauty, Dr Owen and Pete Sampras.

Pete Sampras
Men's Final

Independence [signature]

Lovers cannot help but reveal their sexuality, either through their face or the media.
Beauty and the Beast . . .

David Mellor's full lips and boyish hair make him irresistible.

Bill Clinton's nose and bedroom eyes reveal a strong sexual urge.

Cecil Parkinson, matinée idol looks and smarmed-down hair.

Paddy Ashdown, crinkly eyes and military bearing.

But even the beautiful face can age.

Michael Heseltine

The face of Frank Sinatra, young and old.

There are little things that can be done to fix our faces up, hitch our faces up. It is well nigh impossible to spot a face that has been fixed, apart from a startled look, and the ears being on top of the head.

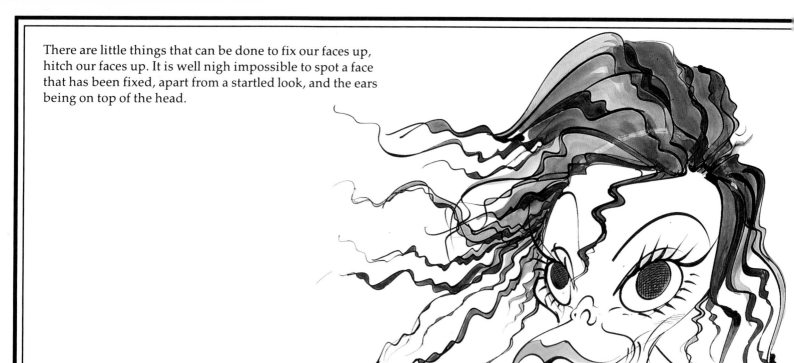

Michael Jackson. A manufactured face.

Nancy Reagan

But cosmetic surgery can have its drawbacks.

An unfortunate incident in Neverland.
Michael Jackson.

mask (1) (mask) [F. *masque*, from Sp. *máscara* (see MASQUERADE) or med. L. *mascus*, *masca*, etym. doubtful], *n.* A covering for the face, for protection or to conceal one's identity; a subterfuge,

Gerald Scarfe

Theatre masks allow actors to perform in ways that would be more embarrassing if they weren't masked, and so with many of us. We wear a mask to hide our true self – we try to present the face we would like people to see. We know we are not really like that.

In some the mask covers vulnerability, in others it is a thin veneer and hides a near animal side to their nature. It is a mask that can cover raw emotions – and the seven deadly sins.

The artist's job is to capture the true character of the face behind the mask. The caricaturist should leap for the jugular with a snarl, tearing away the sophistication and affectation and arriving at the bare bones.

Alec Guinness has no face until he takes a role.

An actor does not necessarily need to hide his face behind a mask of heavy make-up, false nose and wig. He can distort or present his face in such a way as to convince us that what we see is the true character of a face other than his own.

Anthony Sher, Laurence Olivier, Kenneth Branagh

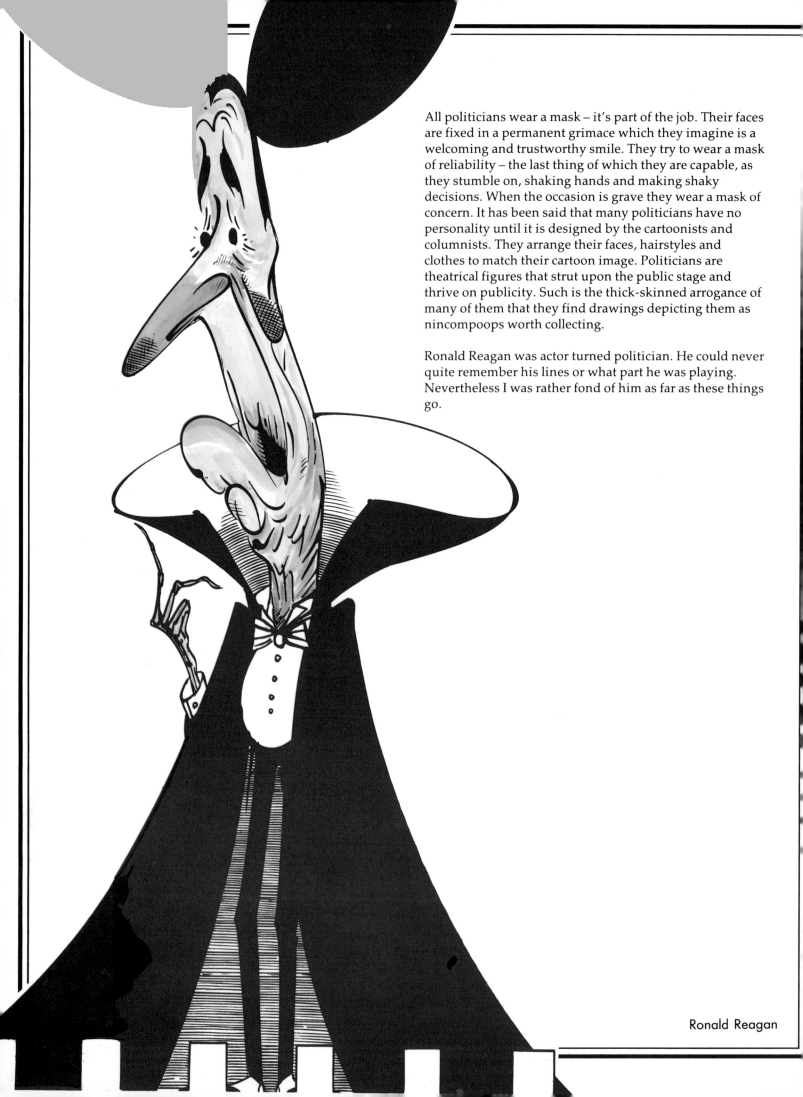

All politicians wear a mask – it's part of the job. Their faces are fixed in a permanent grimace which they imagine is a welcoming and trustworthy smile. They try to wear a mask of reliability – the last thing of which they are capable, as they stumble on, shaking hands and making shaky decisions. When the occasion is grave they wear a mask of concern. It has been said that many politicians have no personality until it is designed by the cartoonists and columnists. They arrange their faces, hairstyles and clothes to match their cartoon image. Politicians are theatrical figures that strut upon the public stage and thrive on publicity. Such is the thick-skinned arrogance of many of them that they find drawings depicting them as nincompoops worth collecting.

Ronald Reagan was actor turned politician. He could never quite remember his lines or what part he was playing. Nevertheless I was rather fond of him as far as these things go.

Ronald Reagan

From the beginning I could not stand Richard Nixon. His mask slipped very early on and I drew him as a real villain long before he drowned in Watergate. His shifty eyes, sweaty upper lip and six o'clock shadow made him a real candidate for a baddie from the beginning. But baddies always make the best subjects, any actor will tell you that, and strangely, when Nixon finally went, I missed him as a subject.

Richard Nixon hides behind the mask of Henry Kissinger.

Ronald Reagan dons the anonymous mask of his Vice President, George Bush.

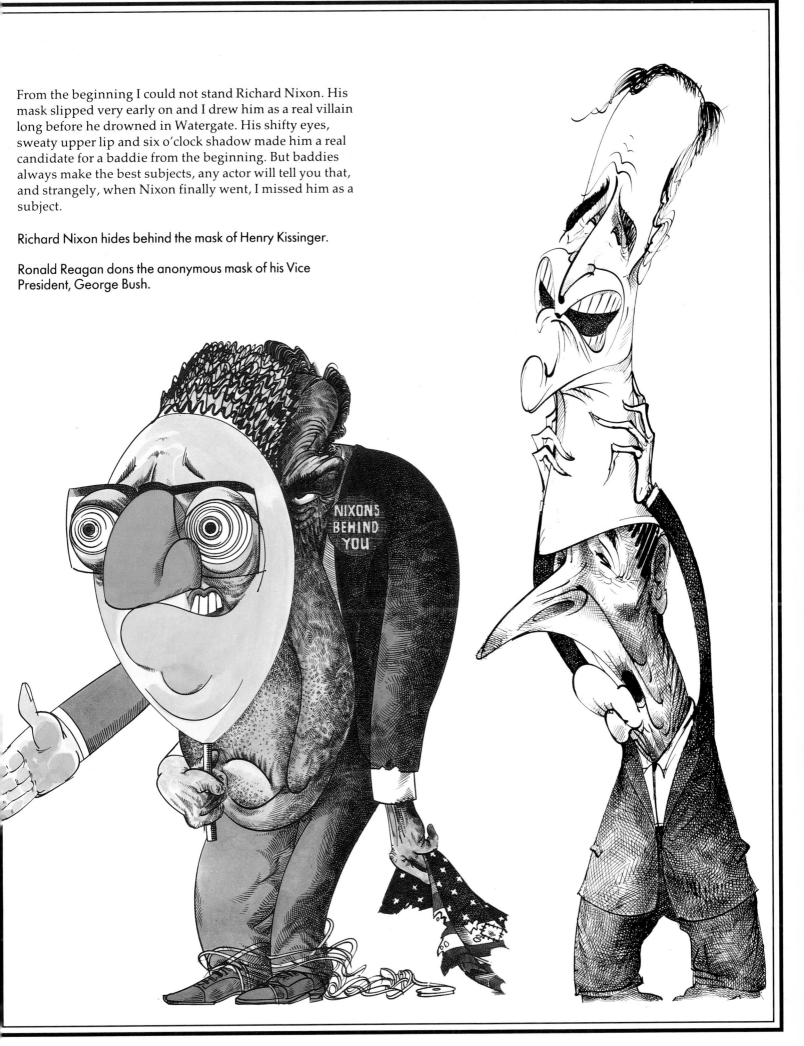

41

MARGARET THATCHER

HAROLD WILSON

EDWARD HEATH

INDUSTRIAL RELATION ACT

Politicians put themselves on pedestals and like to think of themselves as great men and leave us their portraits in oil paint, stone and bronze; images they would like us all to see, the hero, the innovator, the leader of men. In time, when the knives and the memoirs come out, the faces start to crumble.

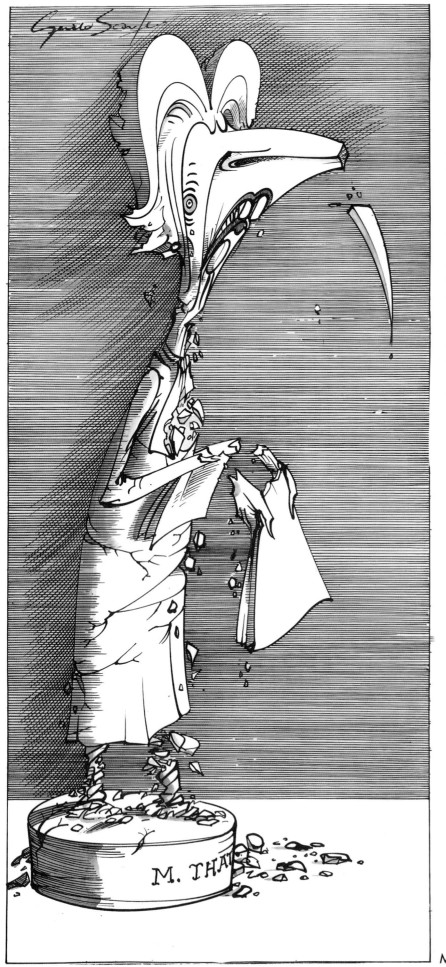

How is the mask stripped away and a true portrait achieved?

A photographer captures a given moment when he thinks his subject is relaxed or off-guard and is showing his or her true persona.

An artist takes apart and reassembles a face onto the canvas, and while doing so allows his thoughts on the subject's character to flood through his every brush stroke.

A caricaturist creates a super-extension of the face and character. He creates a surreal image which convinces the viewer that is how the person really looks, although he knows it to be impossible.

Margaret Thatcher

portrait (pôr' trát) [O.F. *pourtraict*, p.p. of *pour-traire*, to portray], *n*. A likeness or representation of a person or animal, esp. from life; a vivid description; (*fig.*) a type, a similitude.

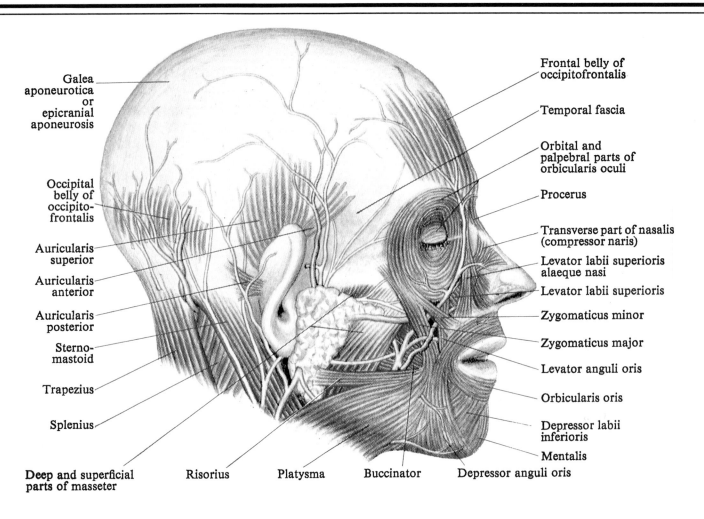

Galea aponeurotica or epicranial aponeurosis

Occipital belly of occipito-frontalis

Auricularis superior

Auricularis anterior

Auricularis posterior

Sterno-mastoid

Trapezius

Splenius

Deep and superficial parts of masseter

Risorius

Platysma

Buccinator

Frontal belly of occipitofrontalis

Temporal fascia

Orbital and palpebral parts of orbicularis oculi

Procerus

Transverse part of nasalis (compressor naris)

Levator labii superioris alaeque nasi

Levator labii superioris

Zygomaticus minor

Zygomaticus major

Levator anguli oris

Orbicularis oris

Depressor labii inferioris

Mentalis

Depressor anguli oris

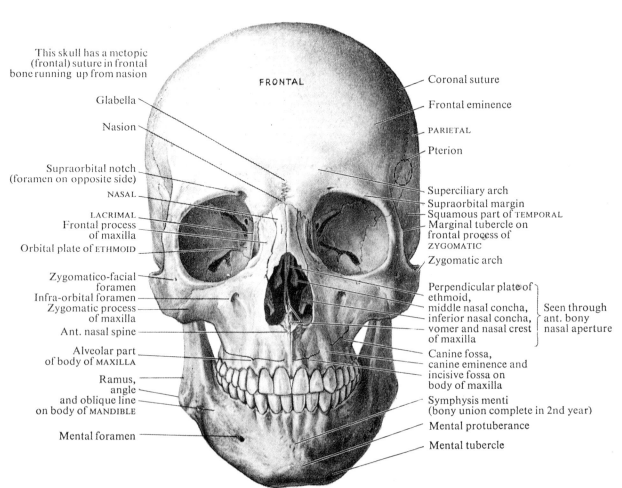

This skull has a metopic (frontal) suture in frontal bone running up from nasion

FRONTAL

Glabella

Nasion

Supraorbital notch (foramen on opposite side)

NASAL

LACRIMAL

Frontal process of maxilla

Orbital plate of ETHMOID

Zygomatico-facial foramen

Infra-orbital foramen

Zygomatic process of maxilla

Ant. nasal spine

Alveolar part of body of MAXILLA

Ramus, angle and oblique line on body of MANDIBLE

Mental foramen

Coronal suture

Frontal eminence

PARIETAL

Pterion

Superciliary arch

Supraorbital margin

Squamous part of TEMPORAL

Marginal tubercle on frontal process of ZYGOMATIC

Zygomatic arch

Perpendicular plate of ethmoid, middle nasal concha, inferior nasal concha, vomer and nasal crest of maxilla

Seen through ant. bony nasal aperture

Canine fossa, canine eminence and incisive fossa on body of maxilla

Symphysis menti (bony union complete in 2nd year)

Mental protuberance

Mental tubercle

anatomy (ă năt′ ȯ mi) [F. *anatomie*, L. *anatomia*, Gr. *anatomia*, abstract n. (*anatomē*, cutting up, from *temnein*, to cut)], *n.* The art of dissecting an organized body so as to discover its structure.

As a teenager and budding artist I felt a desperate need to understand the structure and workings of the face and pored over medical books with the intensity of a student doctor. I slavishly drew in every bone, muscle, sinew and vein. This gave my early drawings a detailed anatomical basis and gained me the reputation of being grotesque. Today my drawings are simpler and more relaxed but I would like to think that they are still based on that anatomical knowledge.

A caricature does not *have* to be anatomically correct as it is not a real representation of that person, it is more of an impression, a reflection, an atmosphere of the subject, but, however much the face is stretched and pulled into an exaggerated likeness, I like to feel that it is based on real flesh, blood and bone and that, distorted as it is, it still has the three-dimensional possibility of living, breathing and moving off the page. A house, however eccentric, will fall down unless it has a solid foundation.

What am I looking for in a face? Where does a portraitist begin? He must draw the atmosphere, the impression and, while elongating on the one hand and truncating on the other, he must still retain the characteristic of the eye, nose, etc. The shape of a Roman nose cannot be made retroussé but its own strong character can be over-emphasised. Everything is an extension, an enlargement or a dimunition of the features. They vie with one another for prominence, for as one enlarges, so must another shrink, otherwise the end result would simply be a larger version of everything.

So ideally I start with an overall impression – a vision. I sometimes see people in my mind's eye as some other being: a parallel apparition with a very strong form, usually exaggerated and sometimes simplified. If I can lash this down onto paper before this wispy apparition dissolves and force it in my direction it results in a parallel idea of that person, something more true than if I had slavishly drawn every feature and wrinkle.

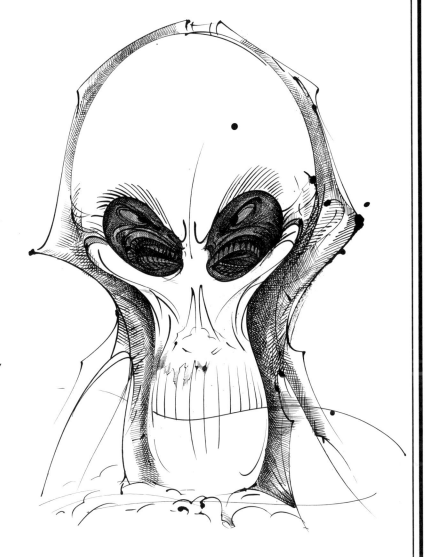

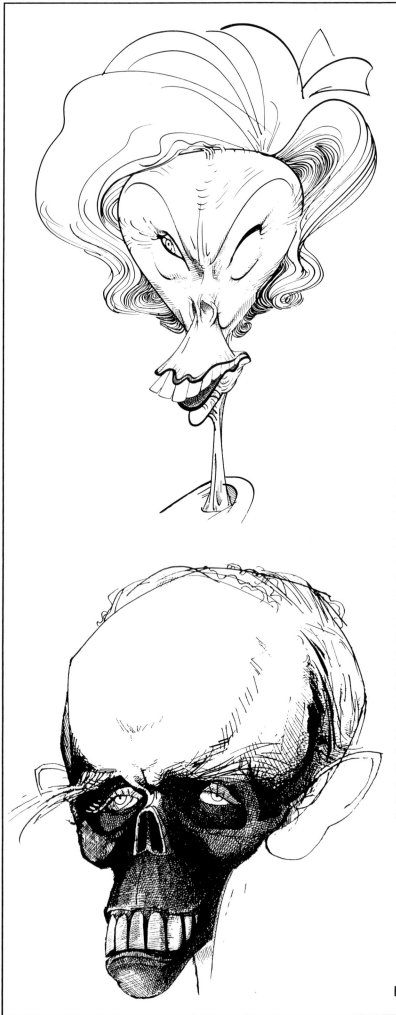

Most portrait painters have to be careful not to offend the sitter. They flatter great mountains of flesh by turning them into presentable, anodyne portraits of people as they would like to see themselves, without warts, and end up with no truth on the canvas at all. They often present an accurate but dead effigy of their subject. The most difficult attribute for an artist to grant his sitter's portrait is the gift of apparent life.

The artists who produce the life-size models for Madame Tussaud's measure the faces of their live subjects to the last millimetre with the result that the wax figures are amazing – just like figures that have been measured to the last millimetre. No magic. Not a breath of life.

The caricaturist's art is to catch his subject on the wing, to capture a look, a glance, a breath, an aroma and an atmosphere – a feeling of that person. He must render it in such a way as to leave room for it to breathe, not set it in concrete and kill it stone dead. Leave an ambiguity, a possibility, a lightness of touch.

Many think if a portrait looks like a photograph it is automatically good – that portrait often says nothing, it adds nothing to the superficial surface view, and presents a mask and not the true character.

I am not interested in making a realistic photographic interpretation. My more realistic sketches are simply grist to the mill, merely notes to be used towards the final caricature. They are jottings that trigger my memory like entries in a diary and summon up a vision that would otherwise have faded.

Picasso was a caricaturist as was El Greco and Modigliani; all drew the face in a stylised way. Picasso tore the face apart and reassembled it in broad cartooned chunks, piled one into the other. El Greco and Modigliani elongated and stretched their portraits. An artist should represent a face in such a way as to make us renew our jaded vision.

Barbara Castle, Lord Home, Michael Heseltine

John Lennon, Ringo Starr,
Paul McCartney, George Harrison

I feel very nervous when I meet a subject and know that I have to capture them on paper. I know that they are nervous too, and don't quite understand what will happen or what they should do. It can be an uneasy experience.

My uneasiness is caused by knowing that I must understand, capture and reproduce their likeness on paper within a short period of time. It is probably the same nerves that an athlete feels when he summons all his knowledge and resources into one given moment. At first my pencil stumbles across the paper, making inarticulate lines that irritate me. But then, gradually, a shape, a pattern, the smatterings of an understanding of that face may dawn on me. It should be easy, the subject sits before me and I simply have to look up to correct any mistakes that I am making.

Although it is important for me to see my subject in the flesh, I prefer to watch them as they go about their normal business. I dislike people sitting for me because I know they will ask to see the sketch and this makes me try to achieve a likeness which will please them. On those occasions when I do show the sitters their caricatures they stare in disbelief. 'Oh well, this is one he definitely hasn't got right. Hasn't got me at all. My nose is not that pointed or my eyes so close together.' It may well be that I haven't captured them, but often their friends can see the likeness.

I take the sketches to my studio and spread them around me, together with any photographs. A terrible tension grows within me, which I will sometimes do anything to avoid. I would rather make a cup of coffee, or sweep the studio floor, than face the drawing board.

There is only one way to release the tension: I must condense the information I have gained about the subject into the purest and simplest form and funnel it onto the paper. Sometimes within two lines I know it will not work. I remove the paper, toss it behind me and immediately begin again, and so on until I feel I am getting somewhere. I do not want to accept the first discovery: there may be more, there always are more, so I push on. I must work at speed otherwise the image evaporates, and if I take a wrong turning I may not be able to get back. Although this pays dividends for a limited succession of drawings, in which I hope I am advancing the spirit and abstract quality of the drawing, if it is not going well I very soon find I have lost the feeling and I am repeating my mistakes and over-simplifying to the point of absurdity. In such cases I often assemble all the right features in what appears to be the correct relationship each to the other and still do not achieve a likeness.

Trying to achieve a perfect and pure line means that I have to be completely accurate because the merest millimetre of a line can spoil the likeness. It is like hitting all the trebles on a dartboard with a continual selection of darts over and over again.

One has to be daring to depart from the known road and strike off up some fascinating and twisting track. I may be rewarded with a delicious triumph but more than often the track ends in a dead-end swamp.

The Beatles on the set of 'Help'. 1967.

ARNIE AT THE
CORONATION OF MARK CANTON
EDEN ROC CAP D'ANTIBES

Drawing Arnold Schwarzenegger – my sons' hero – in Cannes for the *New Yorker* I felt distinctly uncomfortable. Sketching Arnie at six paces feels dangerous – after all he is The Terminator. I showed him the sketch. He looked without expression and after a pause turned slowly towards me and said, without emotion, 'My lips are too big.' Well I wasn't going to argue but back in the studio I made them bigger.

Sketching one of my few heroes – Francis Bacon – in 1967.
His ability to take the face, Magimix it and spread it across
the canvas leaves us stunned – he devours his subject
whole, digests it and spews it out onto the canvas. If
anyone can strip away the mask it is Bacon. He presents
the isolated shuddering in a mass of vulnerable, living
meat.

Francis Bacon 1967.

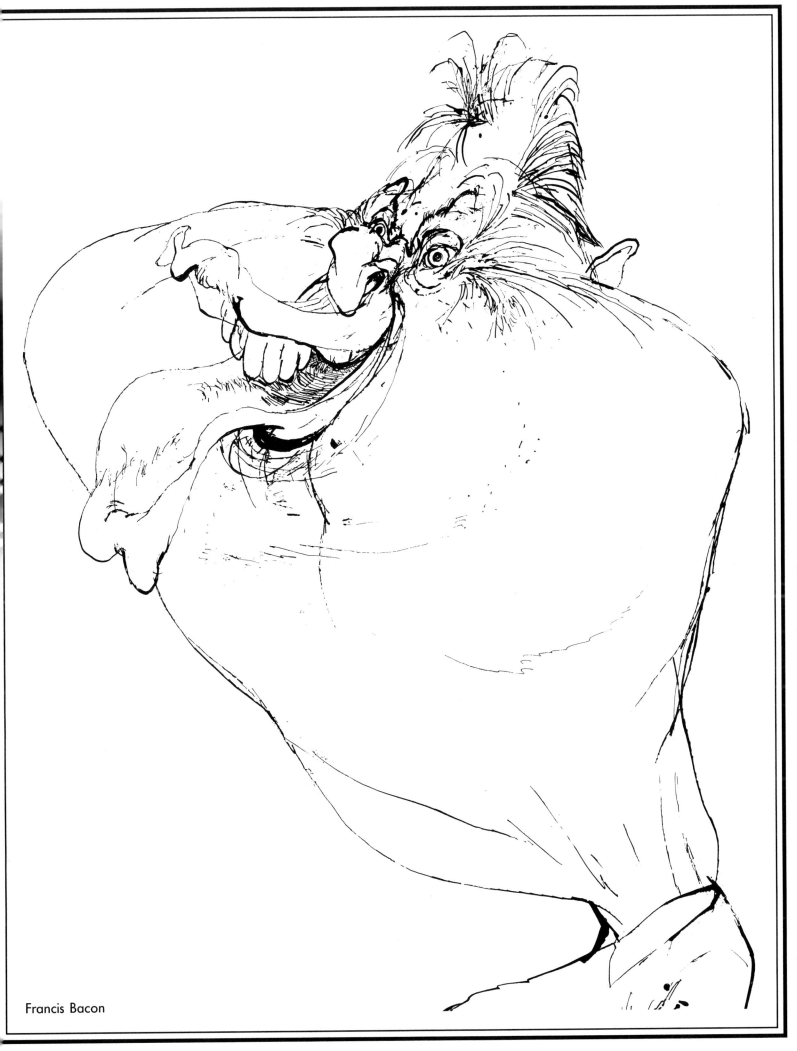

Francis Bacon

55

The face is more than muscle and bone frozen in position; it is a moving spectrum of a million expressions. When we eat, laugh, cry, are angry or sad, the face is never the same for long. It rarely stays immobile unless we are asleep or dead.

Notice the way a perfectly urbane face can be transformed into a bellowing, puce knot of fury, simply by telling him that he has been sacked as Chancellor of the Exchequer. . .

This summer I went for dinner with my family in a hotel in Southwold. We were shown into the parlour where only three tables were set. During the meal I realised that Norman Lamont was at the next table. We ignored one another until the end of the meal, when he introduced himself. We shook hands and exchanged pleasantries.

I tell this slight story because of the feeling of unease I have whenever I meet my victims. Had I been behaving as I normally do to Norman in my drawings, I would have tipped his cauliflower soup all over his carefully coiffed head and rammed his duck up the other end.

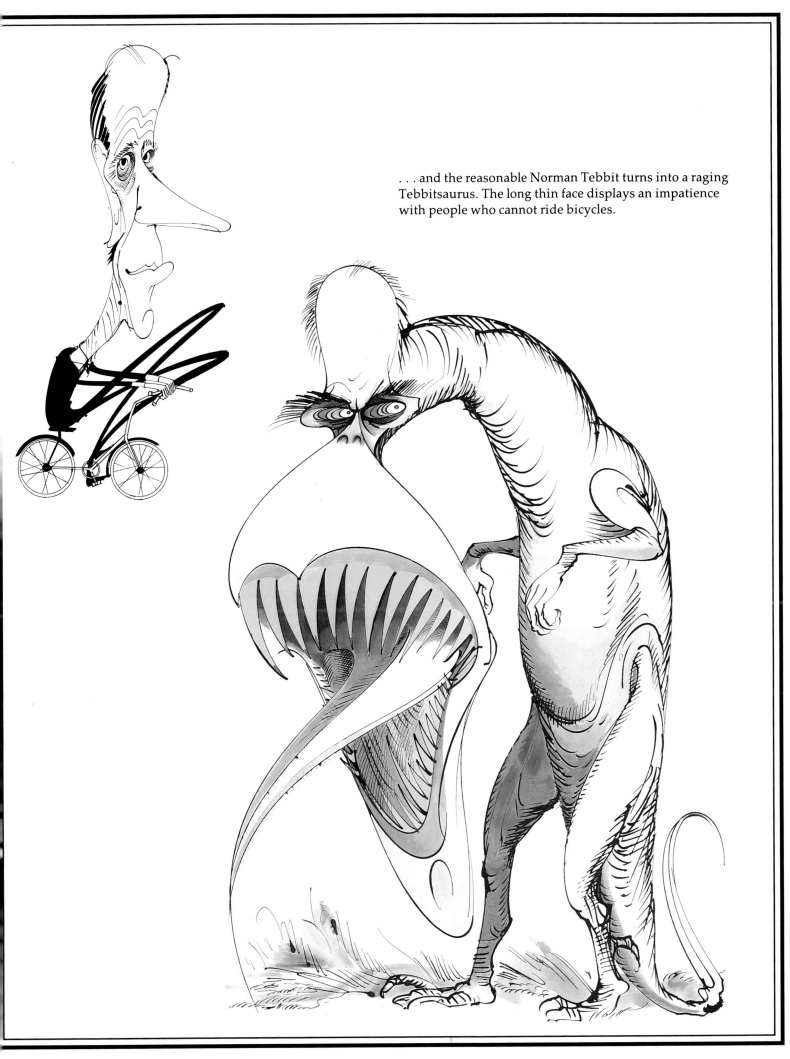

. . . and the reasonable Norman Tebbit turns into a raging Tebbitsaurus. The long thin face displays an impatience with people who cannot ride bicycles.

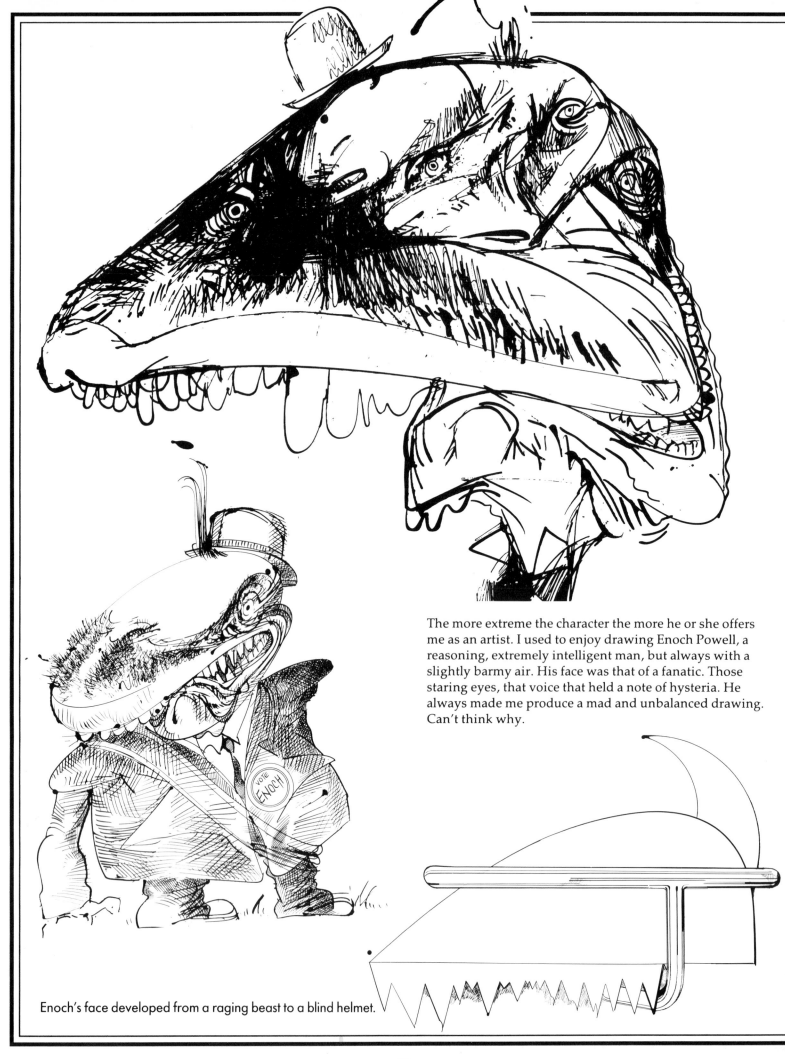

The more extreme the character the more he or she offers me as an artist. I used to enjoy drawing Enoch Powell, a reasoning, extremely intelligent man, but always with a slightly barmy air. His face was that of a fanatic. Those staring eyes, that voice that held a note of hysteria. He always made me produce a mad and unbalanced drawing. Can't think why.

Enoch's face developed from a raging beast to a blind helmet.

ENOCH POWELL: 'A NASTY SHOCK'   1971

John Smith, the exciting face of the Labour party.

John Smith is bad enough, but what can I do with the face of John Major? (Remember him?) Nothing to get hold of. Dull, I should say so. Nice man, but he couldn't even put up a deck chair.

I cannot imagine drawing John Major as anything incisive – as an axe for instance. Even though he may sack a member of his cabinet or cut the old age pension, his character will not allow me to draw him with a cutting edge. A fudger; a muddler. A limp dishcloth – Oh yes, maybe that.

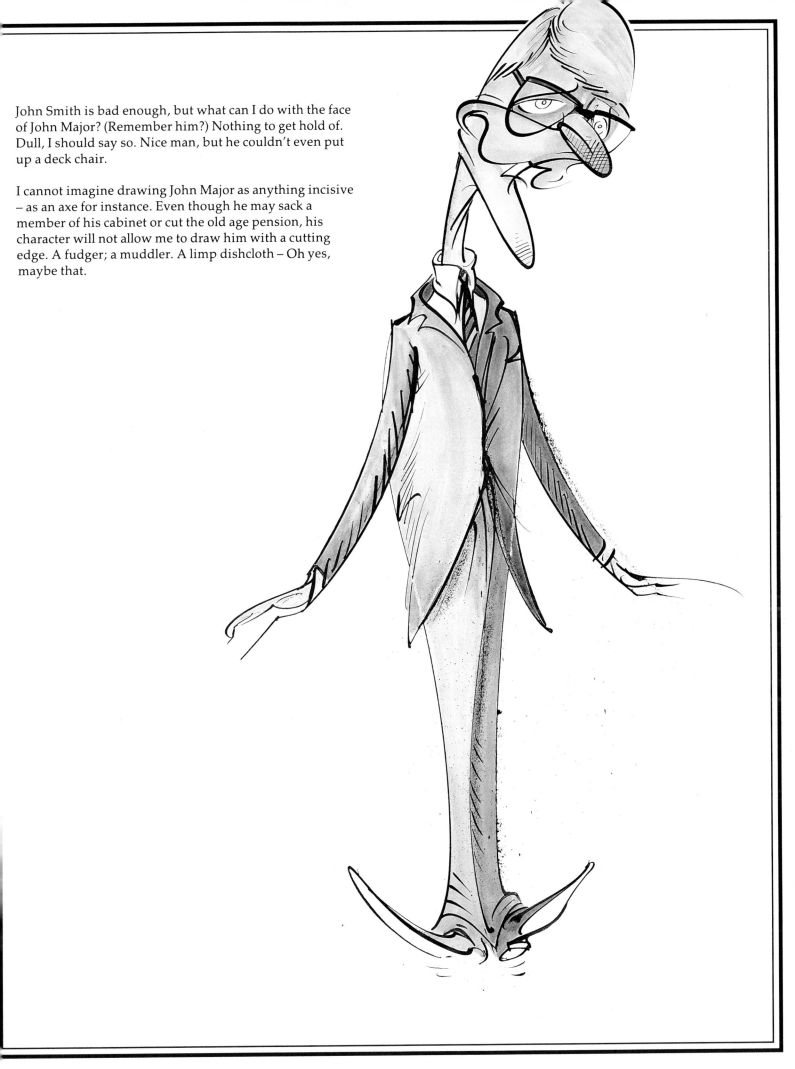

So, given the dire state of the raw material, what can a caricaturist do? Drawing the same characters over and over again can be more than tedious, so I relieve the boredom by turning them into birds or fish or animals. We are all animals after all and the transformation from man to beast is a short step – for some shorter than for others.

John Major makes a rather unsuccessful dodo

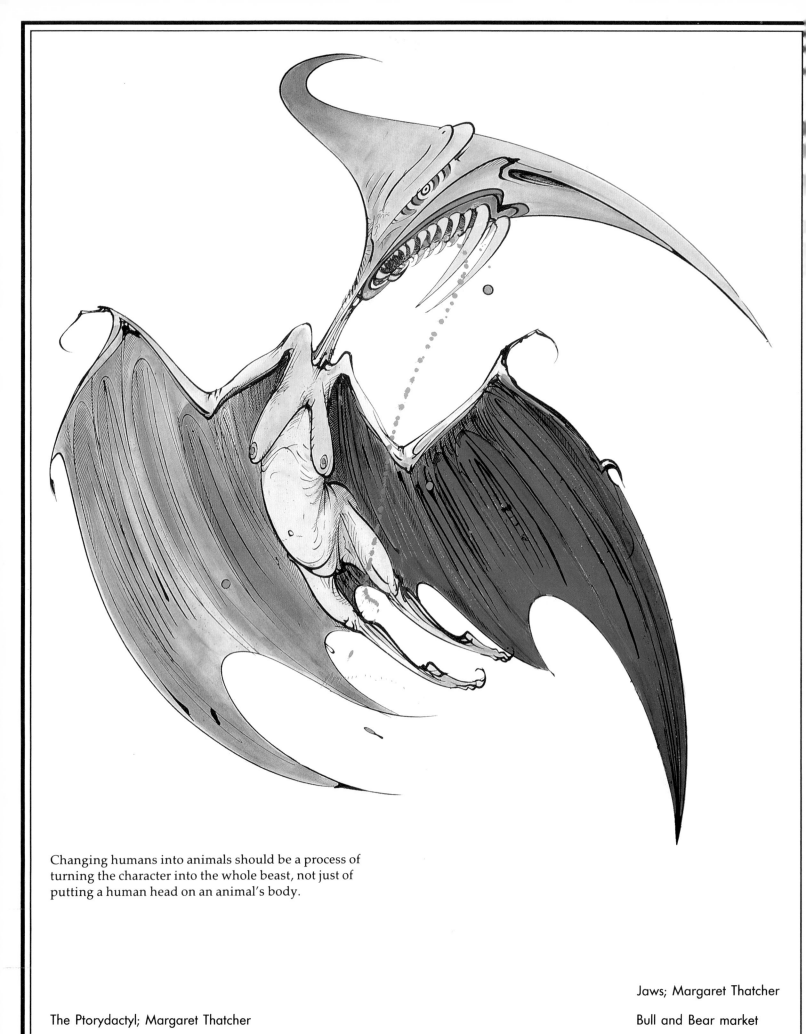

Changing humans into animals should be a process of
turning the character into the whole beast, not just of
putting a human head on an animal's body.

Jaws; Margaret Thatcher

The Ptorydactyl; Margaret Thatcher

Bull and Bear market

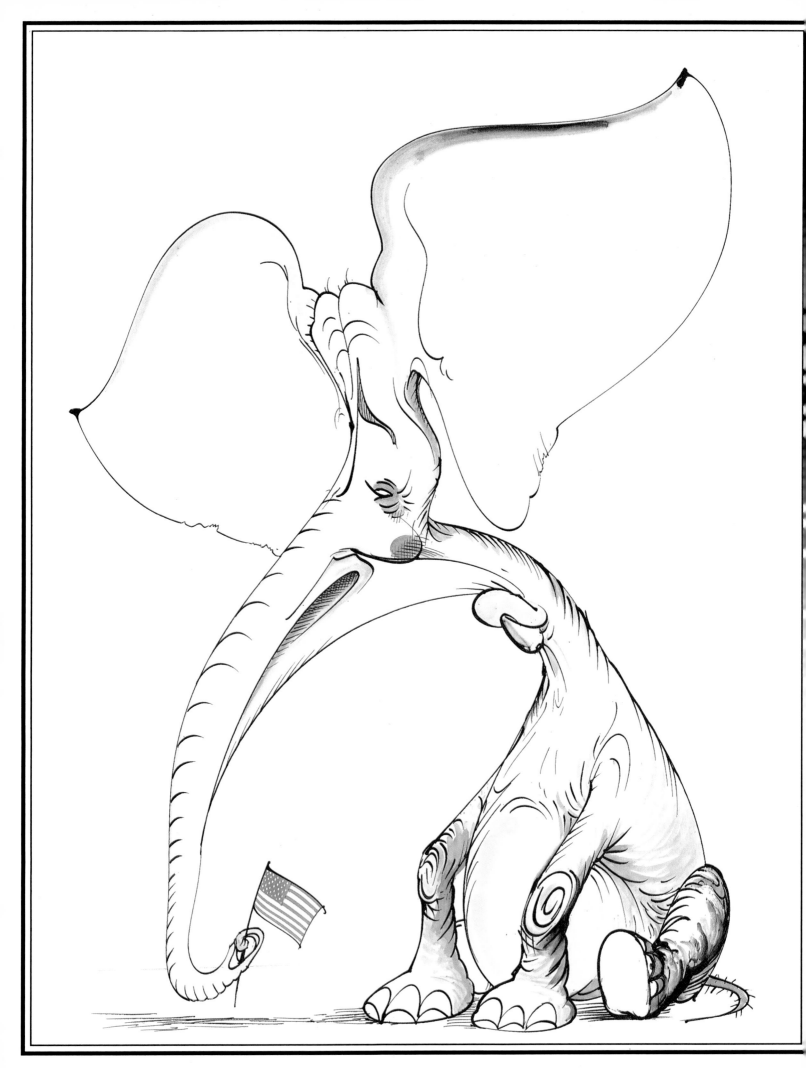

The Mad Cow; Margaret Thatcher
The Royal Lion; the Queen

The Old Republican Elephant; Ronald Reagan

When I tire of turning people into animals then I turn
them into objects.

Are we what we eat?

The unacceptable face of Thatcherism.

Menachem Begin as a desert tank.

President Nixon, composed of and entwined with the Watergate tapes.

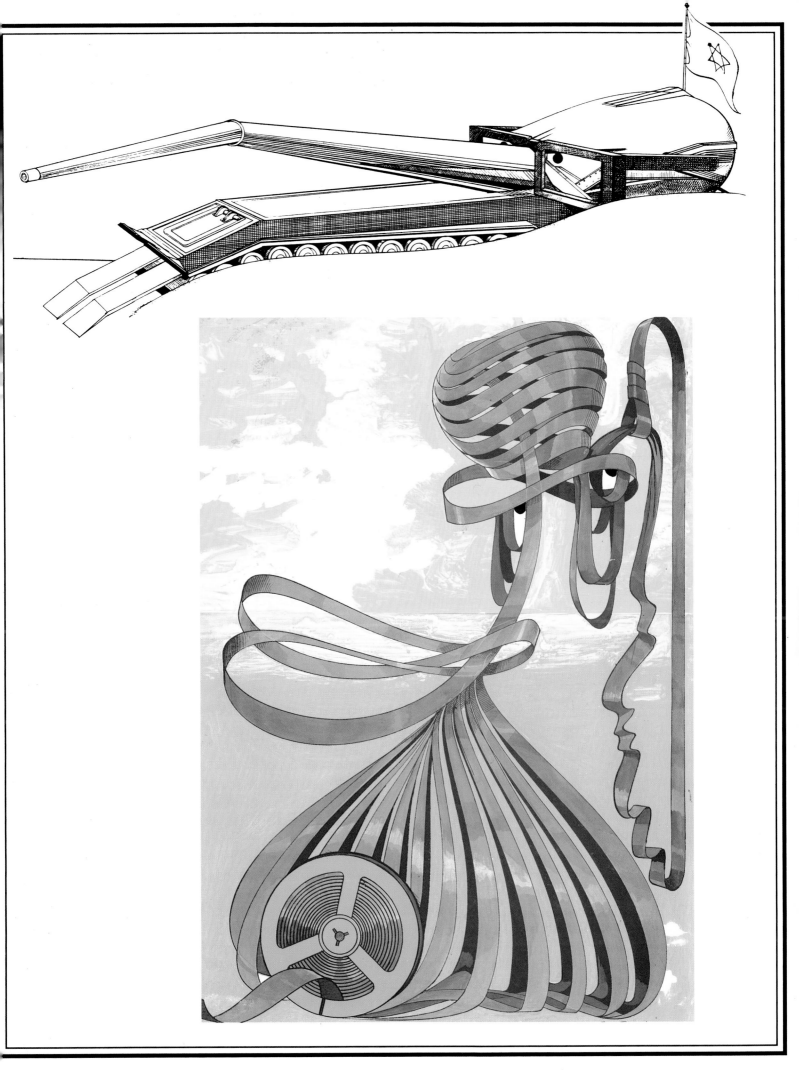

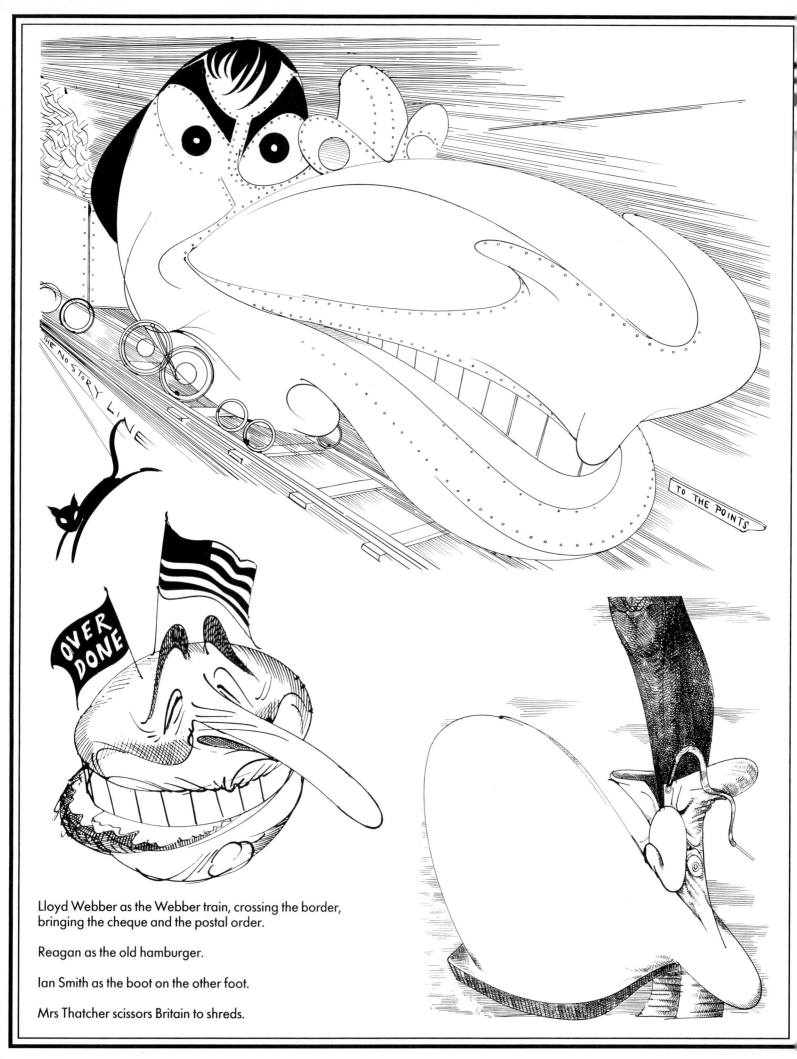

Lloyd Webber as the Webber train, crossing the border, bringing the cheque and the postal order.

Reagan as the old hamburger.

Ian Smith as the boot on the other foot.

Mrs Thatcher scissors Britain to shreds.

Mrs. T. Now there's a face to launch a thousand nibs. In truth her nose is not big but the aggressive, probing, thrusting, cutting, slicing, ever-advancing aquiline nose I gave her seemed to speak of her character. Gradually, in my drawings, she turned from flesh and blood into pure polished, dangerous, unyielding, crushing, cutting metal.

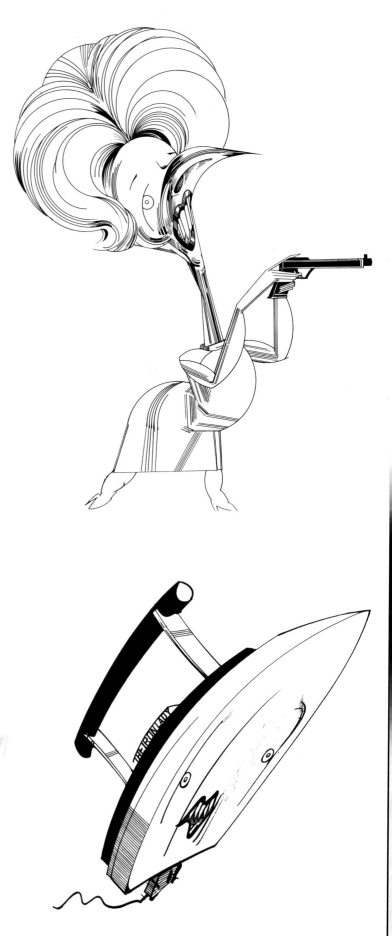

EVER ONWARD

MARGARET THATCHER

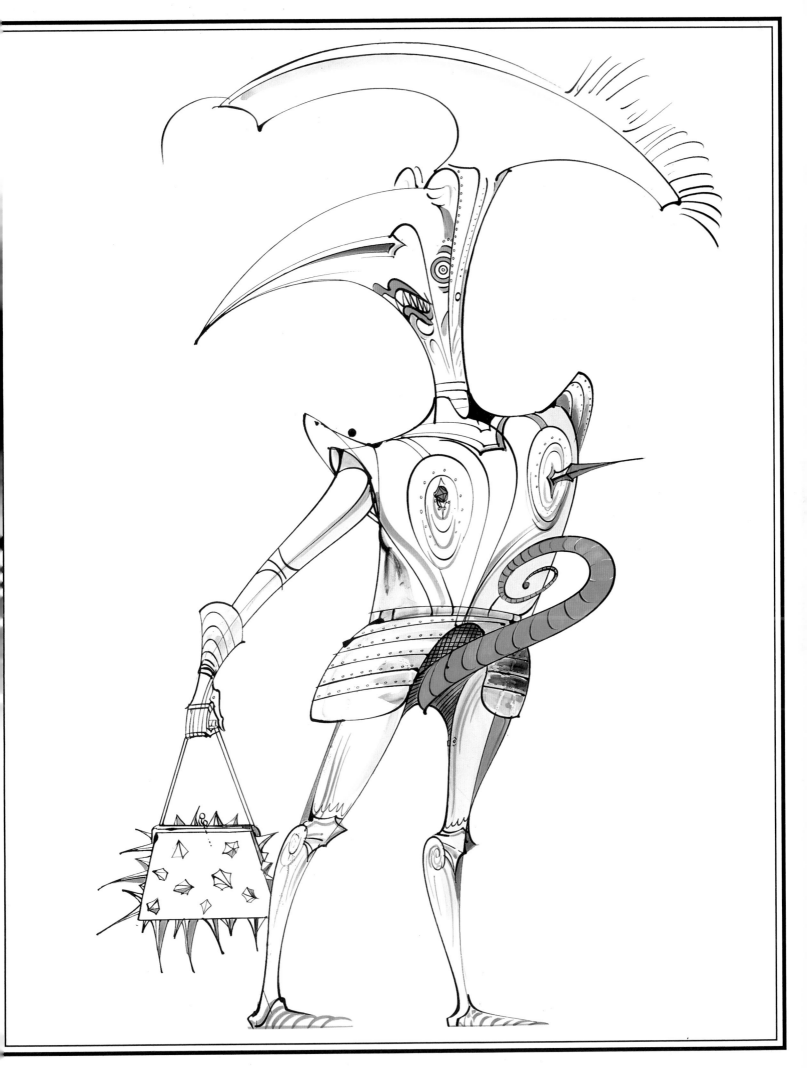

Mrs T. and the unemployed. Finally her face turned into a gigantic axe, cutting her swathe across Britain.

feature (fē′ tyŭr, -chŭr) [O.F. *faiture*, L. *factūra*, from *facere*, to make], *n.* A part of the face, esp. such as gives individual expression and character (*usu. in pl.*); a prominent or distinctive part of anything, a salient point, a striking incident, a mark.

eye (1) (i) [A.-S. *ĕage* (cp. Dut. *oog*, Icel. *auga*, Goth. *augō*, G. *auge*, also L. *oculus*)], *n.* The organ of vision; the eyeball, iris, or pupil; the socket or part of face containing this organ; (*fig.*) sight, ocular perception, view, public observation; perception.

The sly eyes of the old grafter Lyndon Johnson are those of a man not to be trusted.

The old faithful bloodhound eyes of Willie Whitelaw.

Kenneth Clarke's bulging, bullfrog eyes show an optimism against all odds.

Smouldering eyes

Elvis Presley, Michael Howard, Placido Domingo

Norman Lamont

Denis Healey, Susan Sarandon, Joe Gormley.

Eyebrows

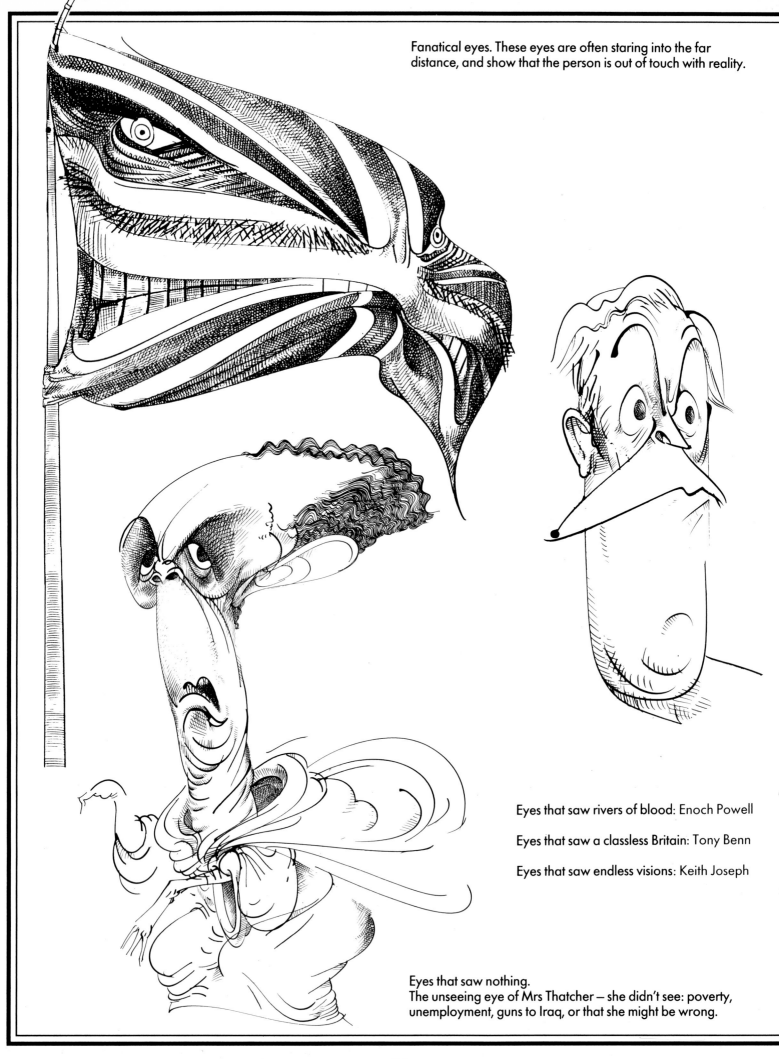

Fanatical eyes. These eyes are often staring into the far distance, and show that the person is out of touch with reality.

Eyes that saw rivers of blood: Enoch Powell

Eyes that saw a classless Britain: Tony Benn

Eyes that saw endless visions: Keith Joseph

Eyes that saw nothing.
The unseeing eye of Mrs Thatcher — she didn't see: poverty, unemployment, guns to Iraq, or that she might be wrong.

nose (nōz) [A.-S. *nosu* (cp. Dut. *neus*, Icel. *nōs*)], *n.*
The projecting part of the face between the fore-
head and mouth. containing the nostrils and the
organ of smell; the power of smelling; sagacity.

Edward Heath

If you see a nose as long as Waldheim's,
it belongs to a liar.

Ed Koch, the mayoral nose.

The nose of a man who twists and turns.
Hugh Scanlon.

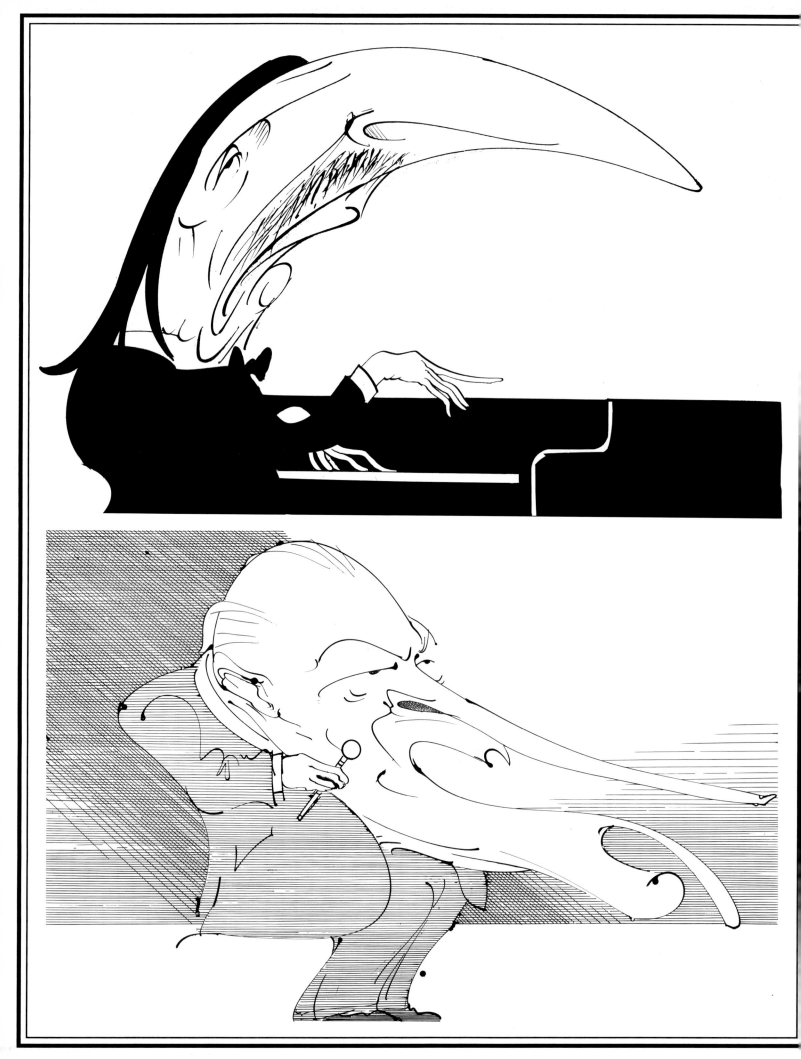

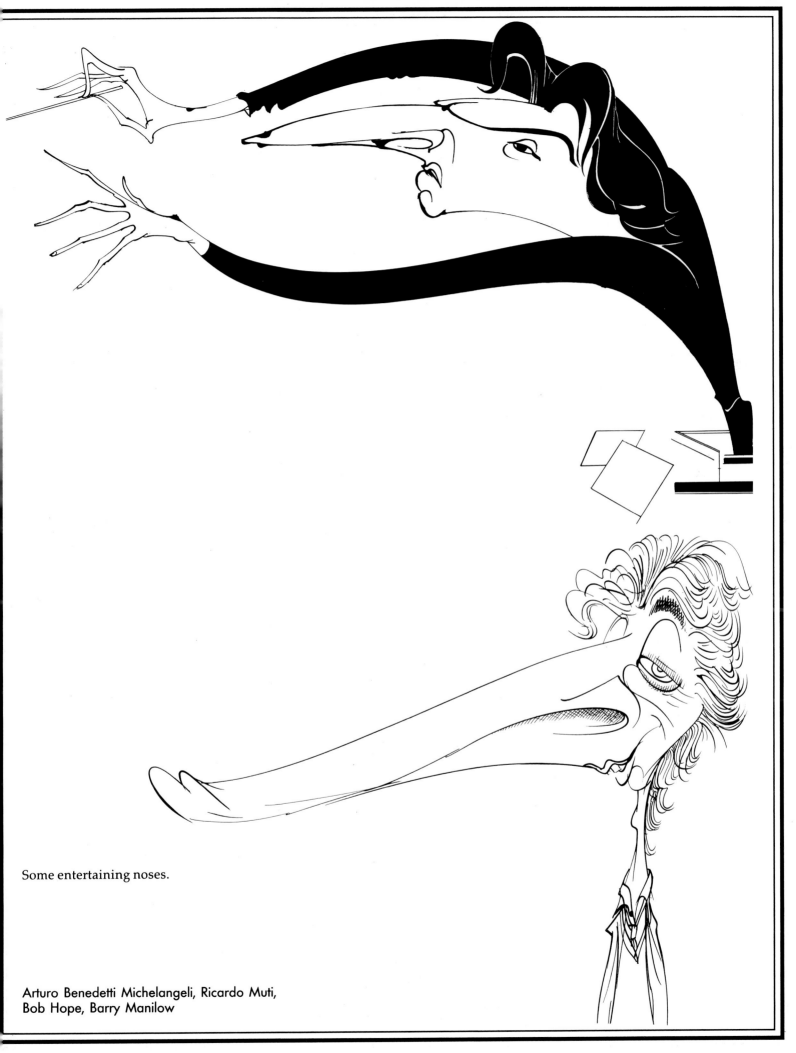

Some entertaining noses.

Arturo Benedetti Michelangeli, Ricardo Muti,
Bob Hope, Barry Manilow

Can you tell class from the face? Is the face of an aristocrat that of a working man with an air of confidence? Would a dustman dressed as a duke look aristocratic? Would a Queen dressed as a tea-lady look lowly? They may be interchangeable, but in general the way of life forms faces. Years of being a social underdog marks the face, just as years of supercilious snobbery and sure fire belief in one's superiority, based on something or other, surely forms a face of towering stupidity.

Tony Benn, Prince Philip,
the Queen, Arthur Scargill

Aristocratic noses.

William Waldegrave, Lord Carrington

Steffi Graf

mouth (mouth) [A.-S. *mūth* (cp. Dut. *mond*, G. *mund*, Icel. *munnr*), cogn. with L. *mentum*, chin], *n.* The opening at which food is taken into the body with the cavity behind containing the organs of mastication and speech; To utter pompously.

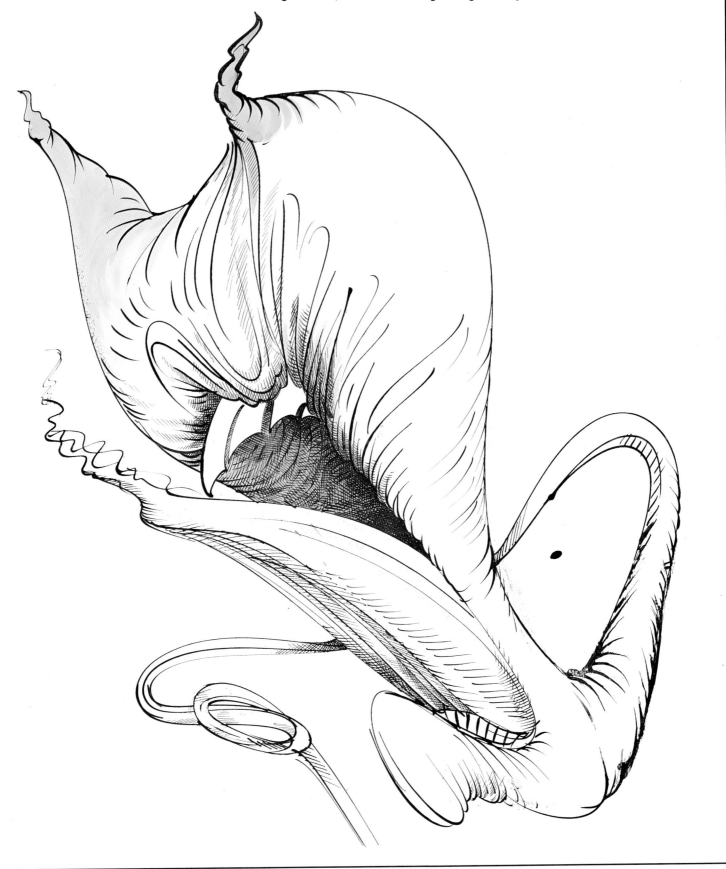

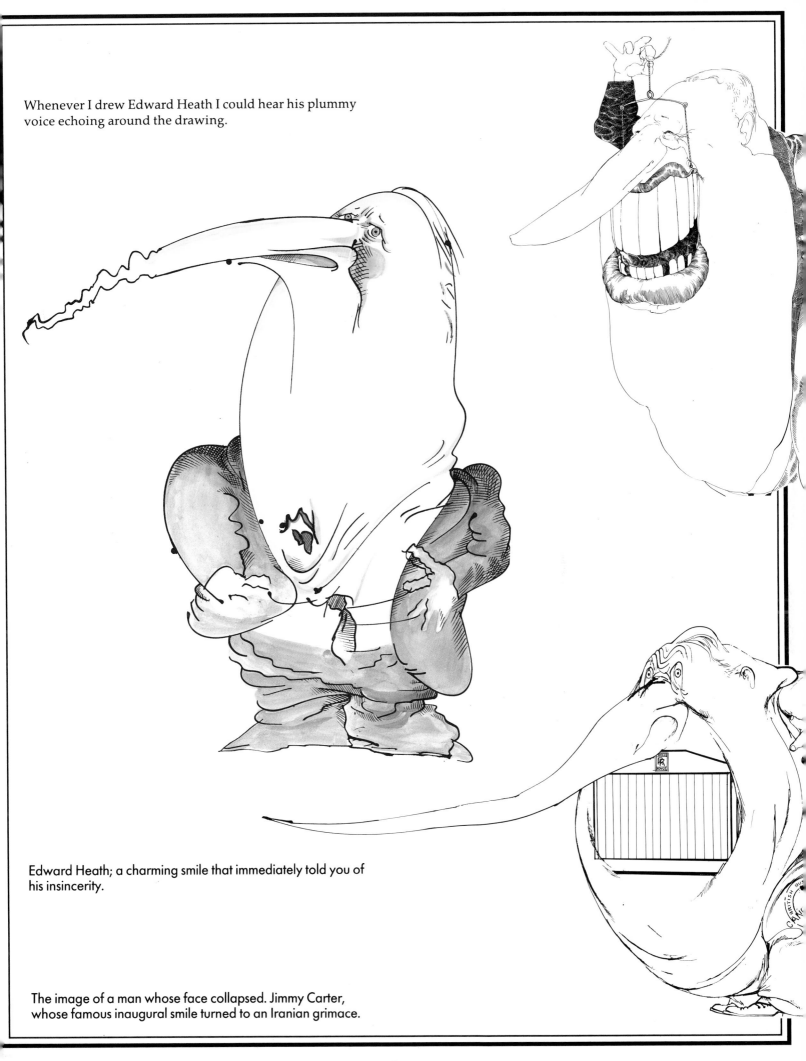

Whenever I drew Edward Heath I could hear his plummy voice echoing around the drawing.

Edward Heath; a charming smile that immediately told you of his insincerity.

The image of a man whose face collapsed. Jimmy Carter, whose famous inaugural smile turned to an Iranian grimace.

tooth (tooth) [A.-S. *tōth*, cp. Dut. *tand*, G. *zahn*, Icel. *tŏnn*, also L. *dens dentis*, Gr. *odous odontos*], *n.* (*pl.* **teeth**) One of the hard dense structures, originating in the epidermis, growing in the mouth.

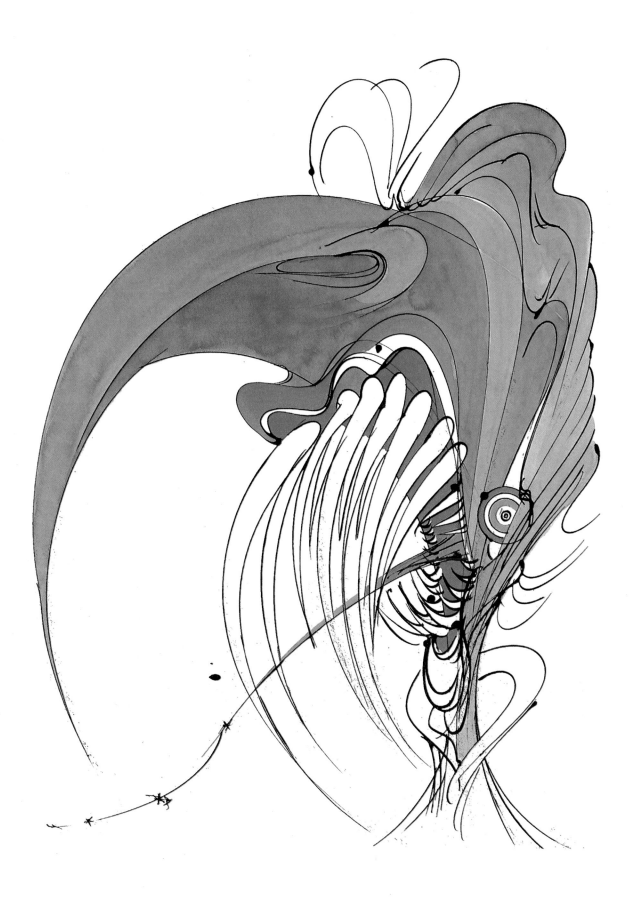

It doesn't pay to stand too close to those who have
predatory teeth.

The fleshy lips of Andrew Lloyd Webber

George Bush. Read my lips, I'm a liar.

Michael Portillo's lips show that he is a high-flier on his way — somewhere or other.

Most people can't get enough of the rhetorical, garrulous lips of Neil Kinnock, as they give forth clouds of lilting, lovely, luxurious Welsh wind.

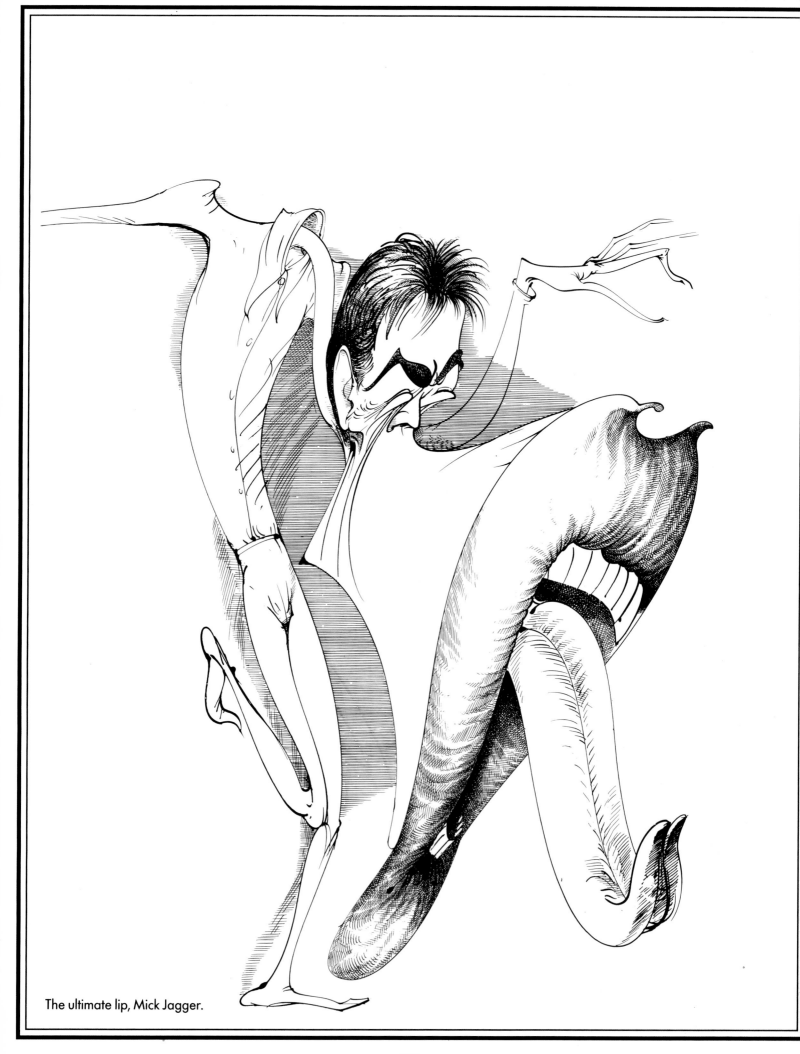

The ultimate lip, Mick Jagger.

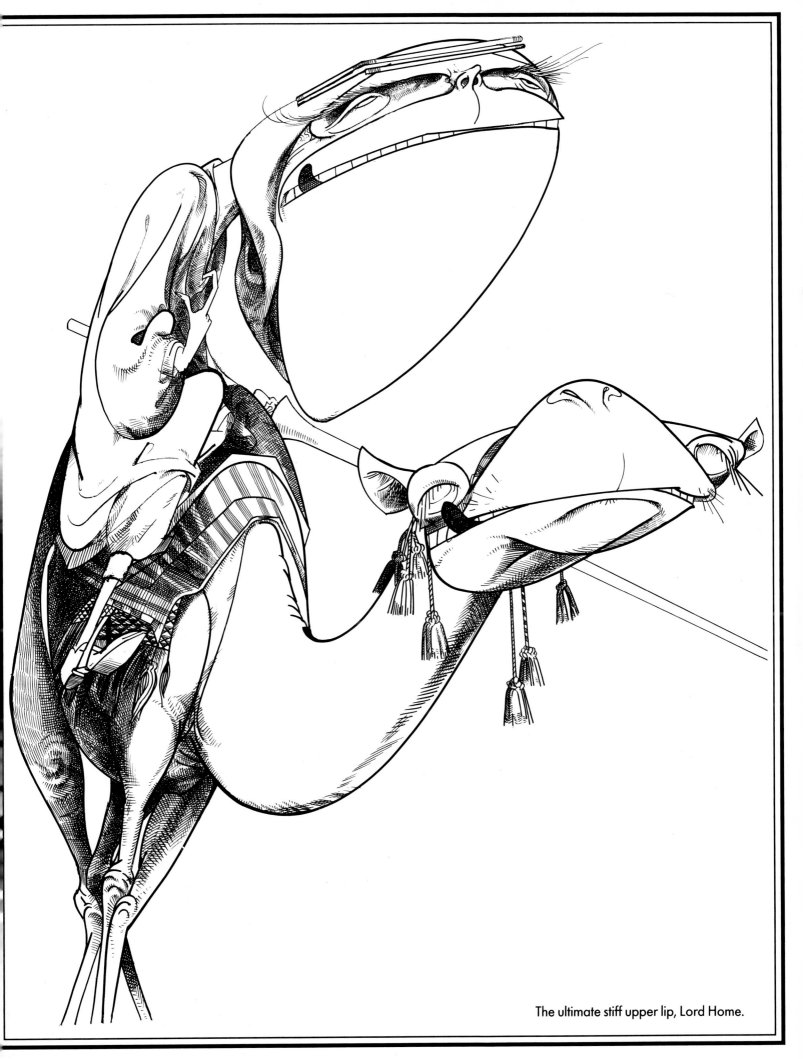

The ultimate stiff upper lip, Lord Home.

Prince, Lulu, Mel Tormé, Tina Turner

Ventriloquist's mouth. Often the person appears to be
talking but is in reality a victim of 'ventriloquist's mouth'.

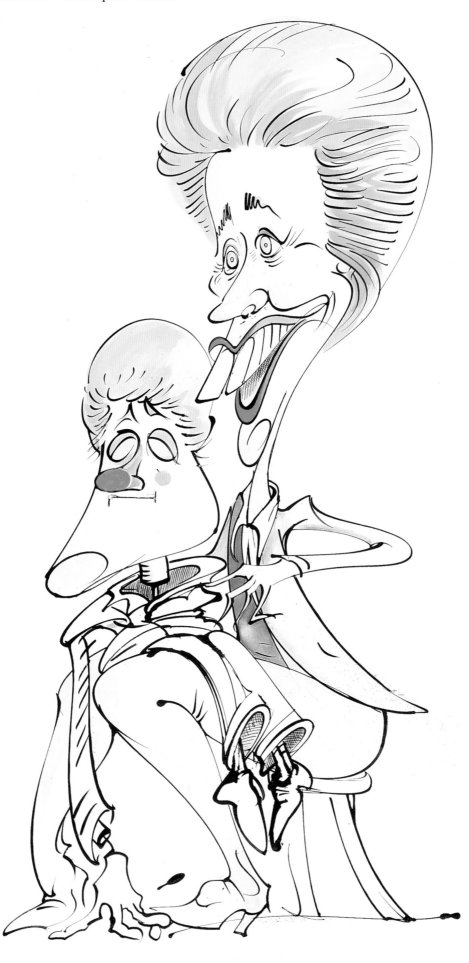

Bill and Hillary Clinton

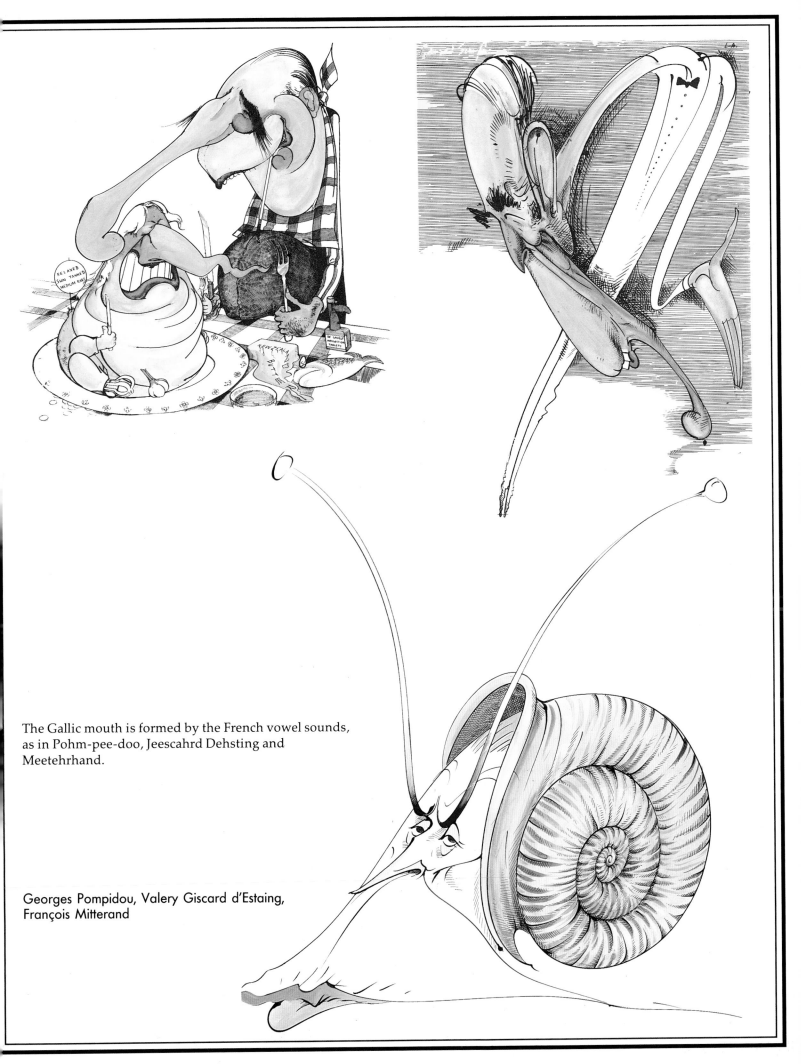

The Gallic mouth is formed by the French vowel sounds, as in Pohm-pee-doo, Jeescahrd Dehsting and Meetehrhand.

Georges Pompidou, Valery Giscard d'Estaing, François Mitterand

chin (chin) [A.-S. *cin* (cp. Dut. *kin*, G. *kinn*, Gr. *geneion*, chin, L. *gena*, cheek)], *n.* The front part of the lower jaw. **chin-wag,** *n.* (*slang*) Chat, talk.

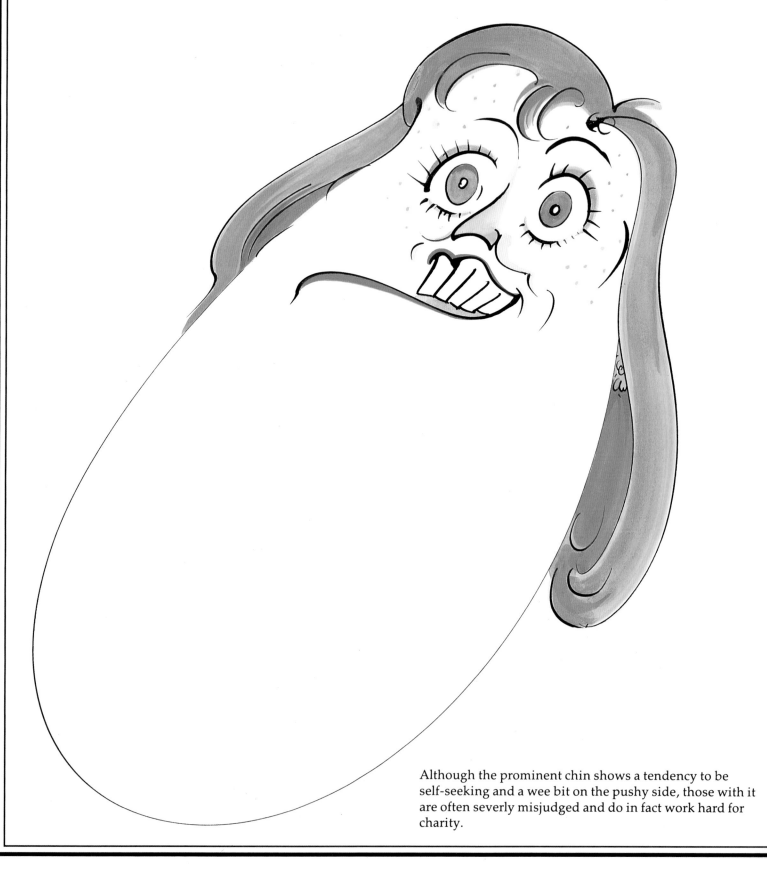

Although the prominent chin shows a tendency to be self-seeking and a wee bit on the pushy side, those with it are often severely misjudged and do in fact work hard for charity.

Duchess of York, Ian Smith

Show business chins.

Daniel Massey, Joyce Grenfell, Peggy Mount,
Griff Rhys Jones,

Leading with the chin. This dominant chin will lead him
to make many mistakes.

Bill Clinton

ear (1) (ēr) [A.-S. *ēare* (cp. Dut. *oor*, Icel. *eyra*, G. *ohr*, L. *auris*, Gr. *ous*)], *n.* The organ of hearing; the external part of this organ; the sense of hearing.

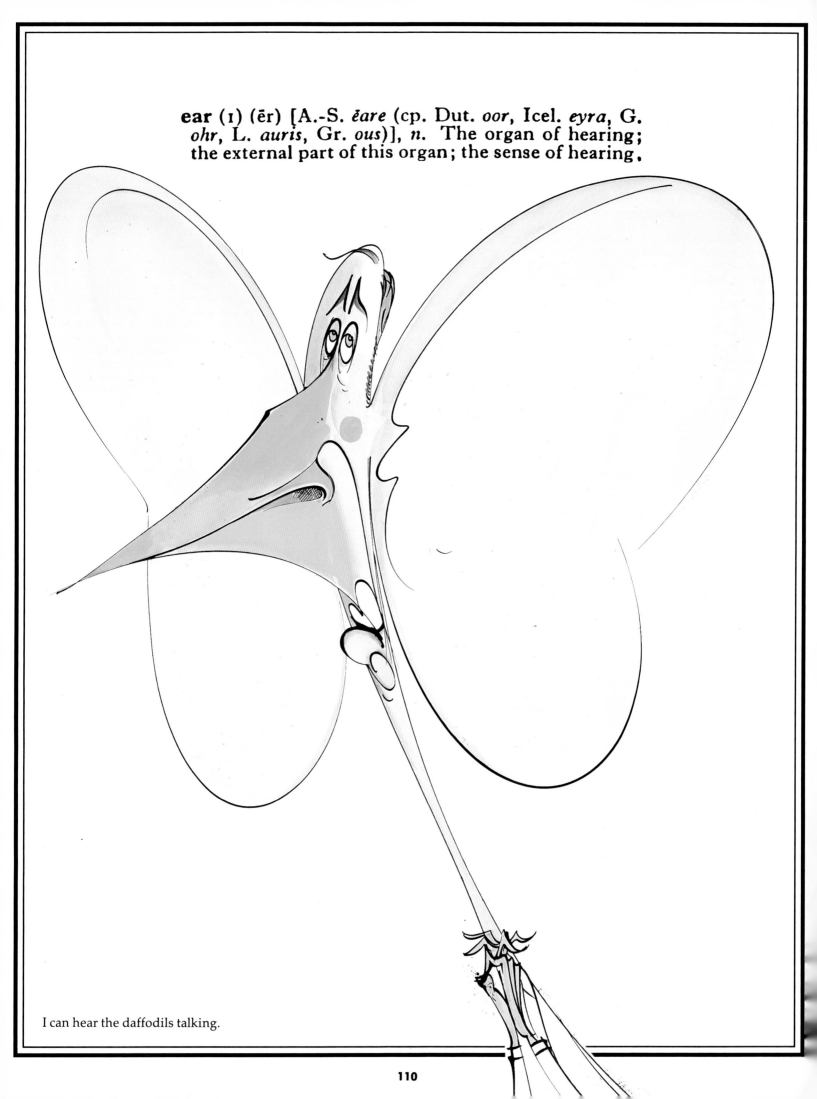

I can hear the daffodils talking.

Large ears usually mean that you are a little bit slow or in some way connected with the royal family.

Princes Charles, Andrew and Edward

The flapping ear: Gerald Ford

The musical ear: Bing Crosby

The listening or Watergate ear: Richard Nixon

Ears of this type give a very strong indication that the character is living in a fantasy world.

Ronald Reagan

hair (hâr) [A.-S. *hǽr, hêr* (cp. Dut. and G. *haar,* Icel. *hār*)], *n.* A filament composed of a tube of horny, fibrous substance. mass of such filaments forming a covering for the head or the whole body.

Zandra Rhodes is trying to attract attention.

Guiseppe Sinopoli, Artistic hair

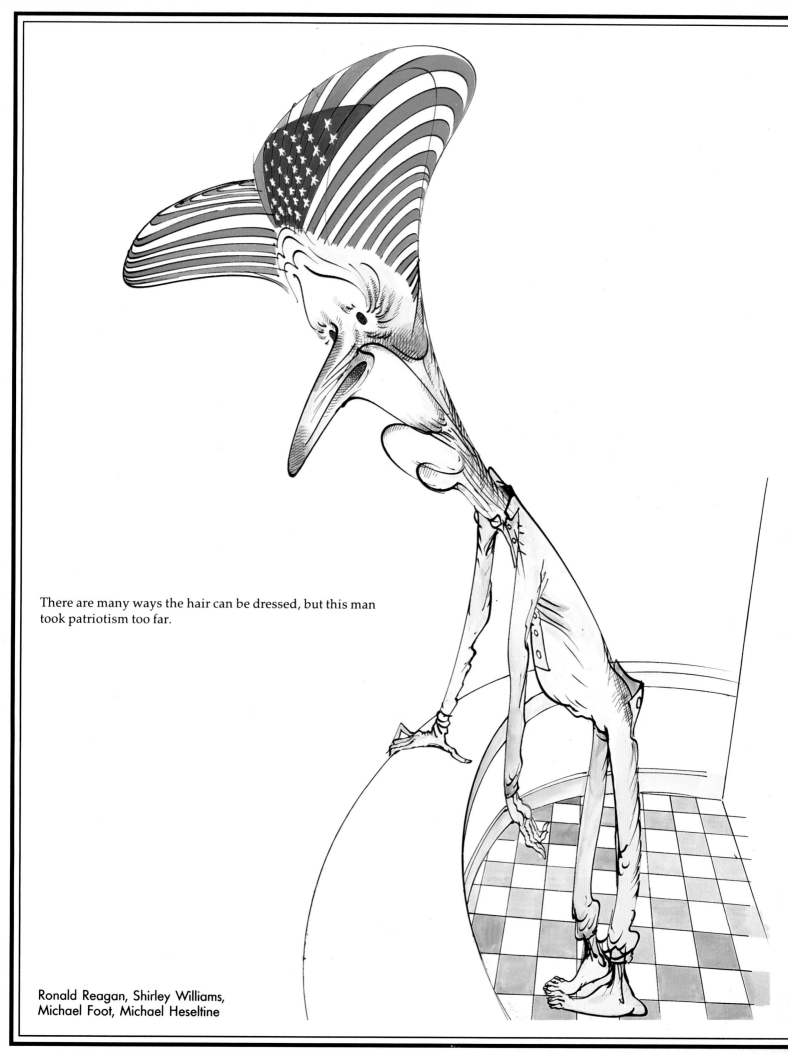

There are many ways the hair can be dressed, but this man took patriotism too far.

Ronald Reagan, Shirley Williams,
Michael Foot, Michael Heseltine

Wild hair.

This is the hair of a man who doesn't quite know what he is doing with his hair. John Patten.

Michael Portillo wanted to improve his image and changed his hair to be more media-friendly. You can see what an improvement it is.

The designer stubble or unshaven chin. This is done to
attract the opposite sex or the media.

André Agassi, Barbra Streisand (nose), Bob Geldof

Lord Longford. A hair line which shows him to be a little on the eccentric side.

Neil Kinnock. The hair of a man capable of leadership.

Arthur Scargill. Hinged hair showing a passionate and friendly nature.

FRAGILE

Sade and Michael Clark

123

jowl (joul) [M.E. *chowl, chavel,* A.-S. *cēafl,* jaw, blended obscurely with M.E. *cholle,* A.-S. *ceolur,* throat], *n.* The jaw; the cheek; the throat or neck, esp. of a double-chinned person; the dewlap.

Norman Willis.

Jeremy Thorpe. The jowls of a clown.

This jowl is the result of saying 'Titter ye not!' too many times.
Frankie Howerd.

The Hanoverian jowl denotes a generous nature, one which opens one's home to anyone (£8).

The more I drew Nixon's face, the more his jowls sagged until one day they separated completely from his face and fell to the ground.

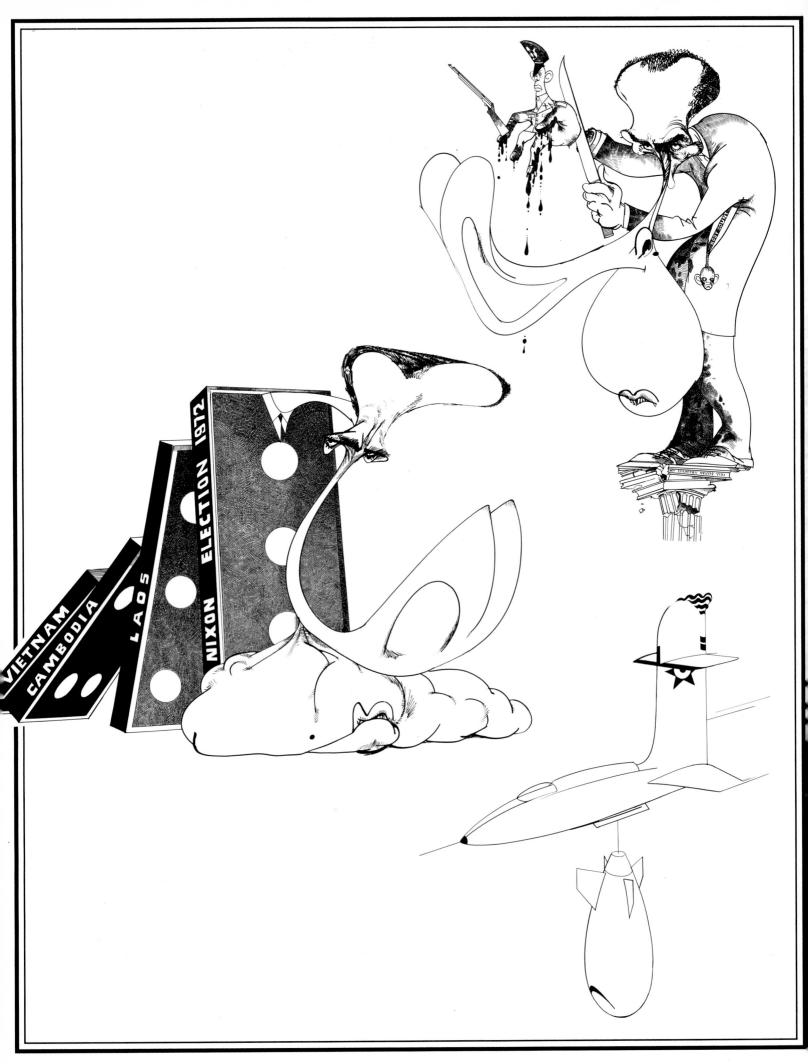

type (tip) [F., from L. *typum*, nom. *-us*, Gr. *tupos*, blow, stamp, character, from *tuptein*, to strike], *n.* A distinguishing mark, a symbol, an emblem, an image; any person or thing that stands as an illus-

phlegmatic, (fleg măt′ ik), *a.* Cool, sluggish, self-possessed, morbid, apathetic, unemotional. **phlegm** (flem), of the four humours of the body.

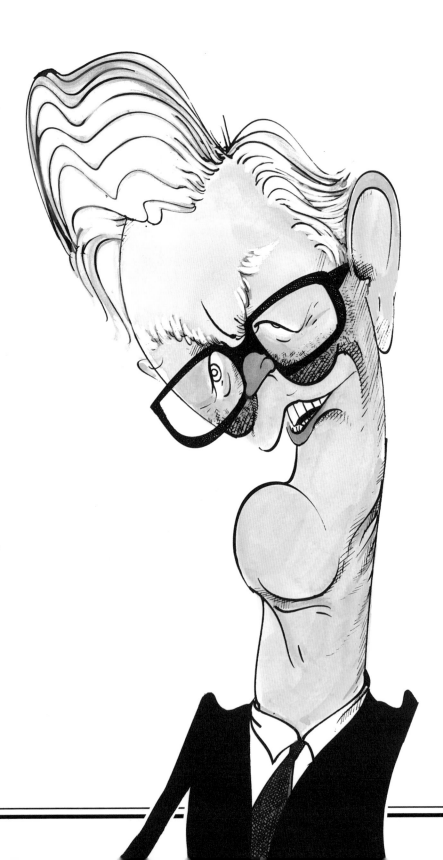

Douglas Hurd, Geoffrey Howe

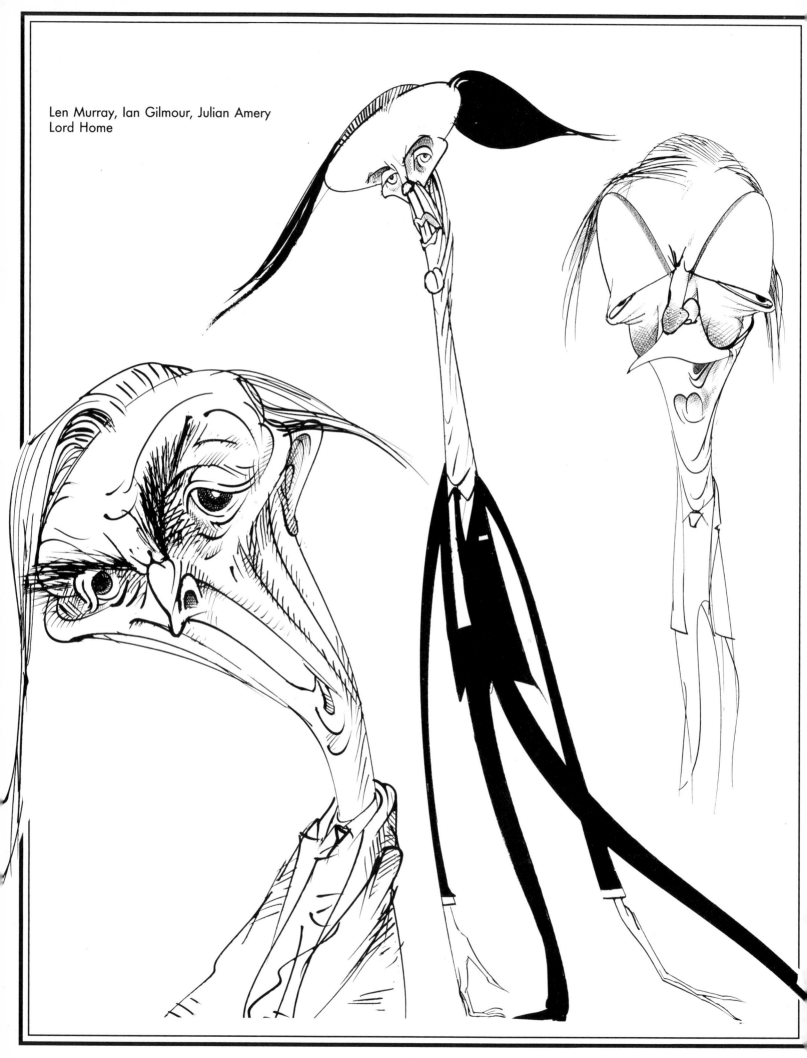

Len Murray, Ian Gilmour, Julian Amery
Lord Home

Phlegmatic pontificators.

John Gummer, Norman St. John Stevas, Gore Vidal
Huw Weldon, Malcolm Muggeridge,
William Rees-Mogg, Paul Johnson

melancholic (mel' ån kól ic) gloomy, dejected
gloomy, depressed in spirits, mournful, black.

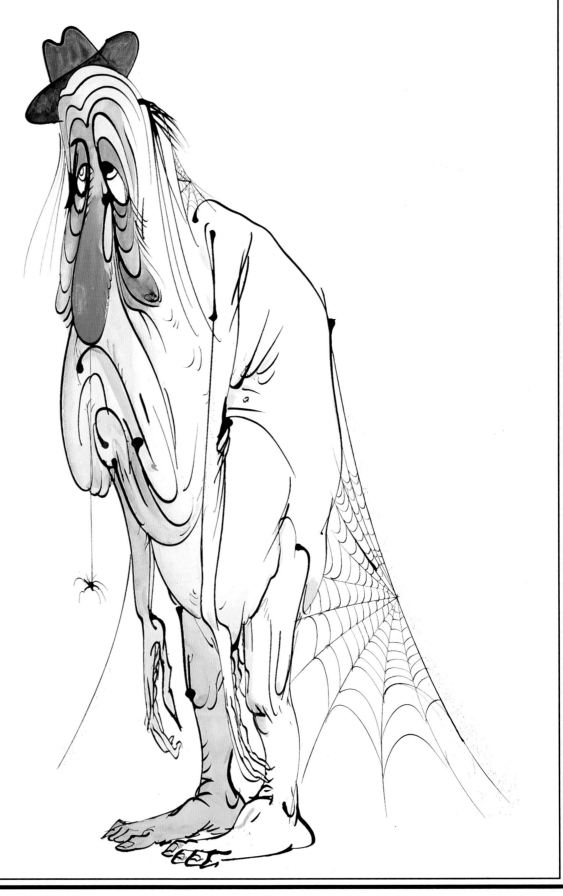

George Bush, Al Gore

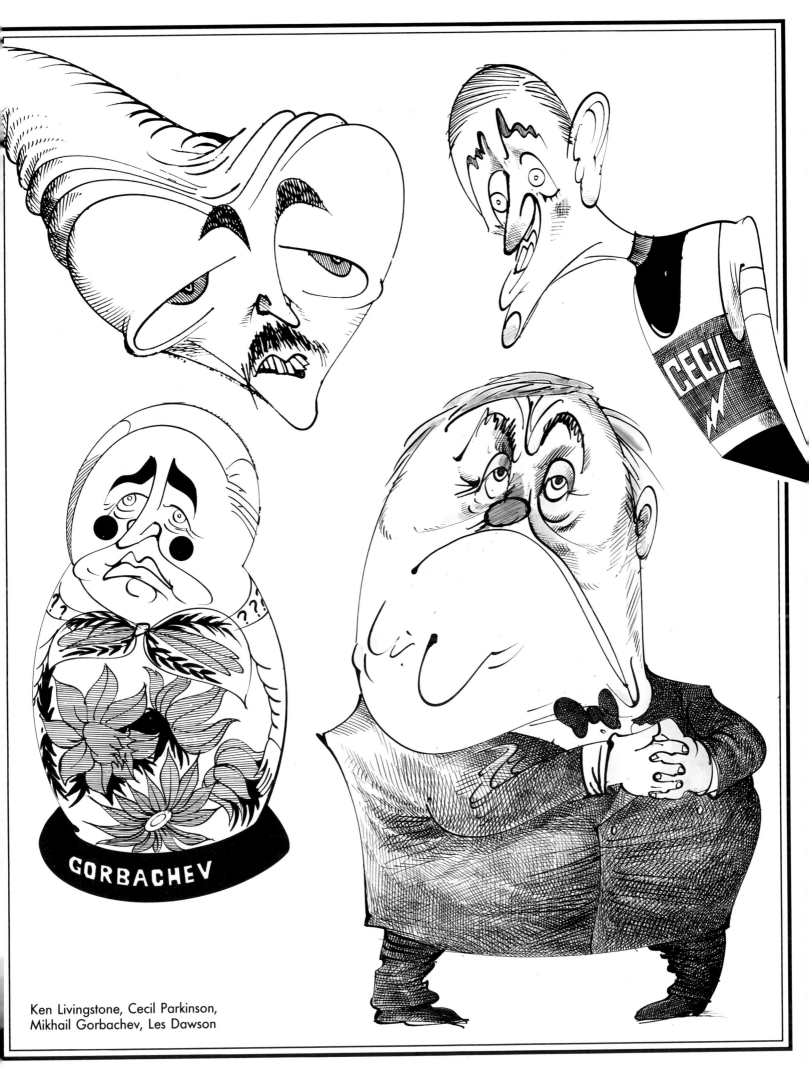

Ken Livingstone, Cecil Parkinson,
Mikhail Gorbachev, Les Dawson

Woody Allen, Philip Larkin

choleric, (kol´ ėr ic) *a.* Full of choler, bile, irascibility, tendency to anger, temper.

Evelyn Waugh, Jeremy Isaacs, Albert Finney,
Glenda Jackson, Mike Tyson, Beethoven

Michael Heseltine, Clive Jenkins

David Owen, Rowan Atkinson

Prince Philip, Boris Yeltsin, Denis Thatcher

Nicholas Ridley, Robert Maxwell

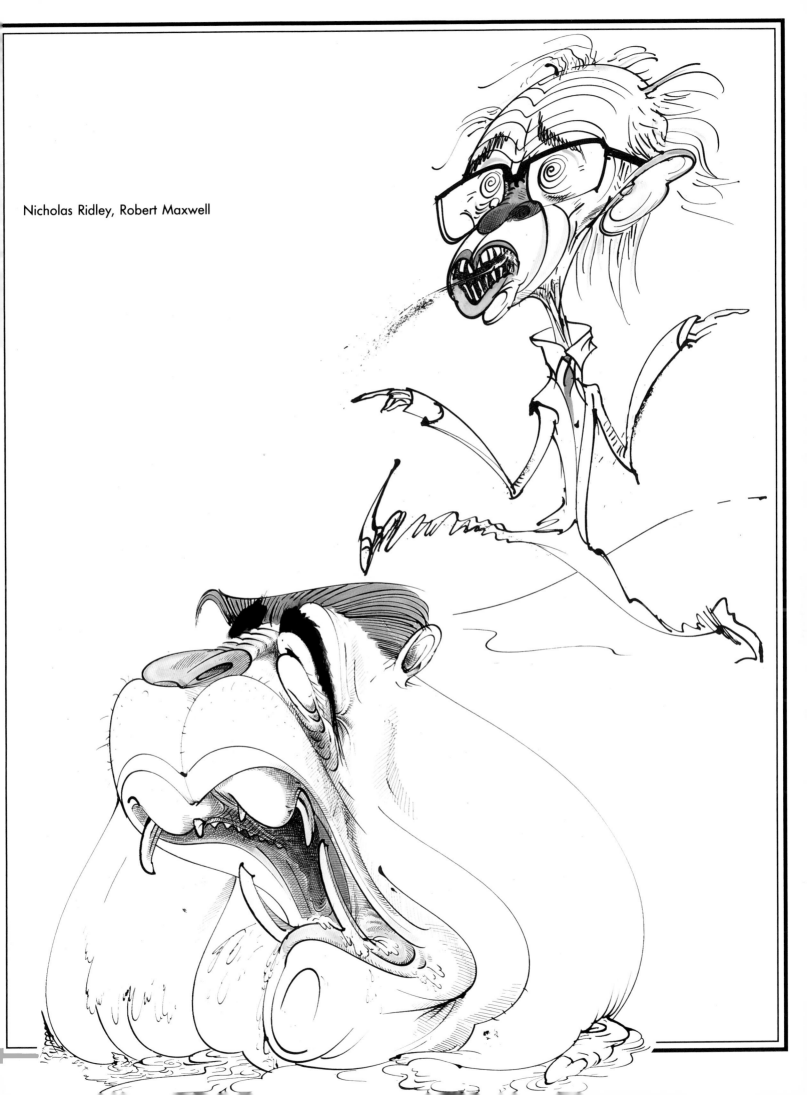

sanguinic (săng' gwin'ik), ruddy, florid, ardent,
cheerful, confident, optimistic, enthusiastic.

Donald Sinden, Lord Beaverbrook

Roy Hattersley, Cyril Smith.
The good claret face, Roy Jenkins.

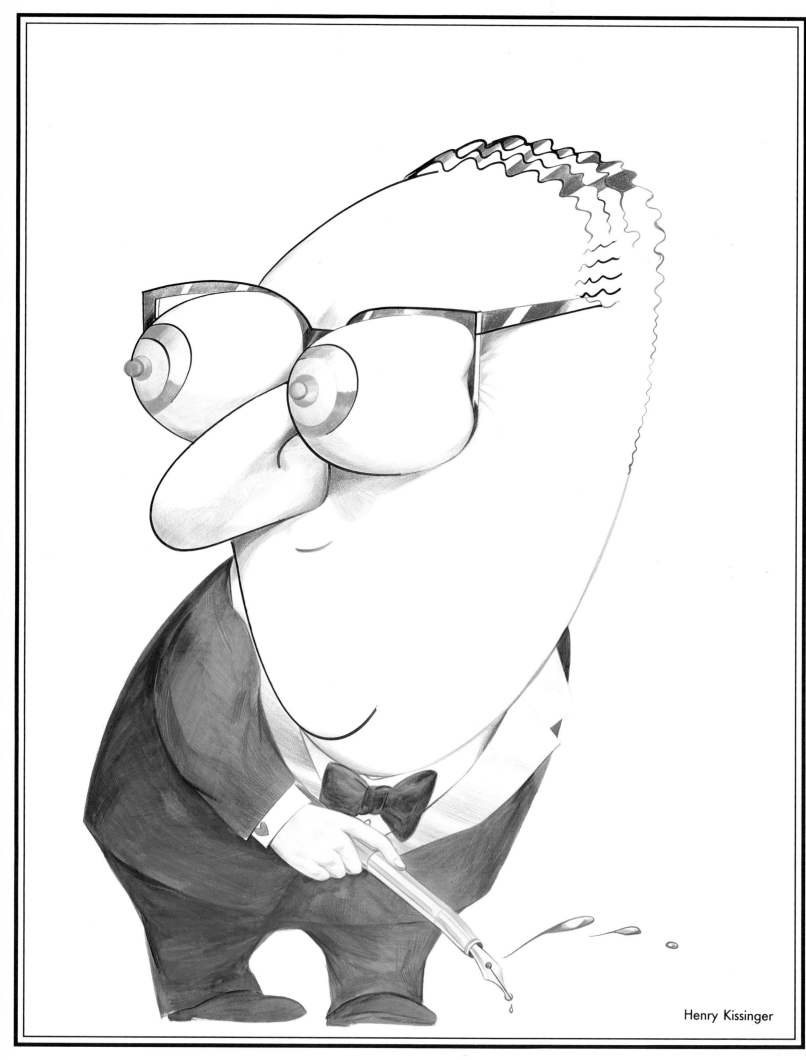

Henry Kissinger

Kenneth Clarke

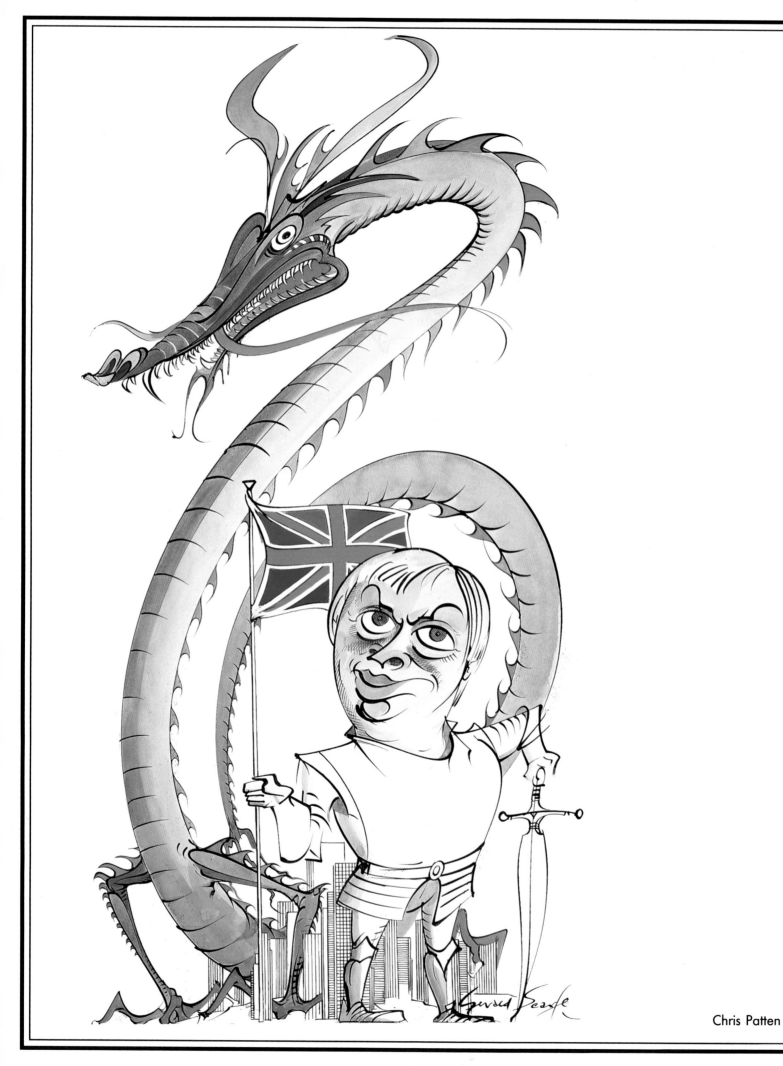

Chris Patten

age (āj) [O.F. *aage*, *edage*, late L. *ætāticum* (L. *ætas* -*atis*, from *ævitas ævum*, an age)], *n.* A period of existence, duration of existence, a period or stage of life, the latter portion of life, senility; maturity.

Deng Xiaoping, the Queen Mother

The Sixth Age shifts into lean and slippered pantaloon . . .

Ronald Reagan

The ageing face on facing age collapses into a crumpled head of sagging flesh and wrinkles.

Margaret Thatcher

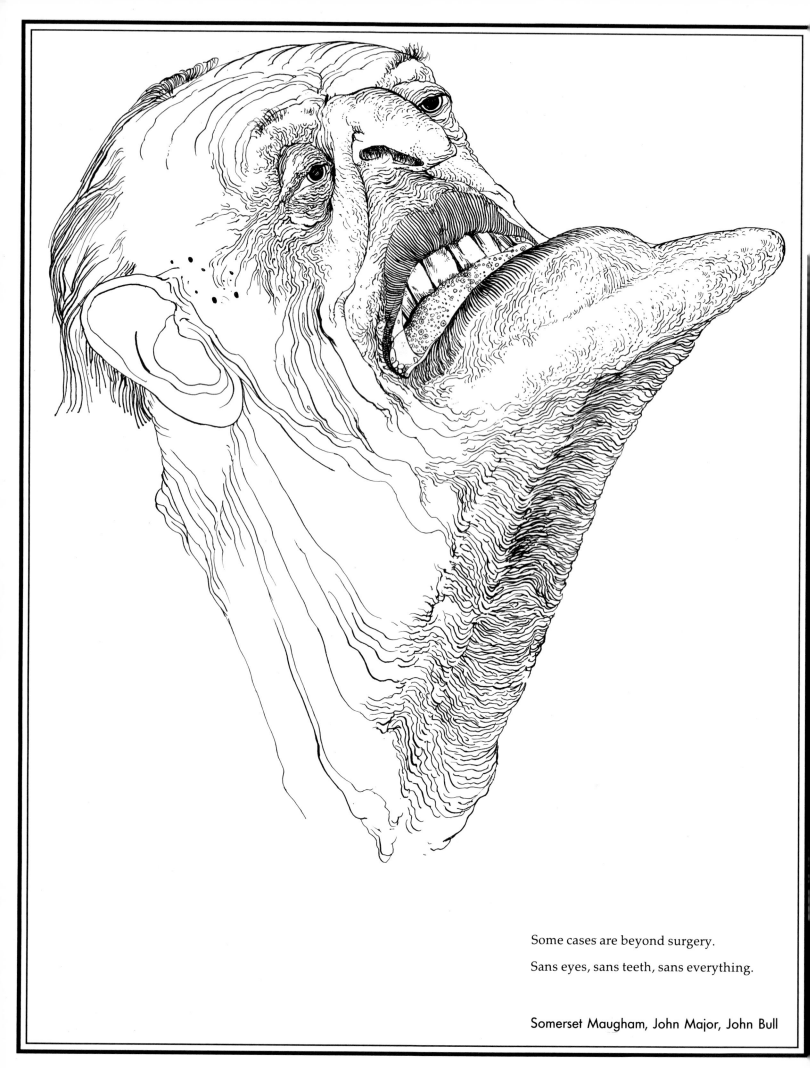

Some cases are beyond surgery.

Sans eyes, sans teeth, sans everything.

Somerset Maugham, John Major, John Bull

Some of these drawings were commissioned by:
the BBC, the English National Opera,
the Guthrie Theatre, Michigan,
the New Yorker, OUI Magazine, Private Eye,
the Royal Court Theatre, the Sunday Times
and Condé Nast Traveler

Arnold Schwarzenegger (inflatable)